Grammar Report

Books For Life Foundation

MARK SHAW

Books By Mark Shaw

Book Report

Grammar Report

Poetry Report

No Peace For The Wicked

Let The Good Times Roll

From Birdies To Bunkers

Code Of Silence

**Miscarriage of Justice,
The Jonathan Pollard Story**

Larry Legend

Testament To Courage

Forever Flying

Bury Me In A Pot Bunker

Jack Nicklaus, Golf's Greatest Champion

The Perfect Yankee

Diamonds In The Rough

Down For The Count

Grammar Report

Basic Writing Tools for Aspiring Authors and Poets

Includes Grammar Grabbers, Punctuation Pointers and Writing Samples

MARK SHAW

Contributing Editors
J. Heidi Newman
Christina Williams

Publisher's Cataloging—In—Publication Data

Mark Shaw 1945—

Grammar Report, Basic Writing Tools For Aspiring Authors and Poets by Mark Shaw
p. cm.

ISBN 0-9717596-4-2

1. *Shaw, Mark 1945— .*
2. *Book Publishing*
3. *Authors and Poets*
4. *Writing Skills*
5. *I. Shaw, Mark II. Title*

10 9 8 7 6 5 4 3 2 1

Printed in the United States of America

If there is a book that you want to read, and it hasn't been written yet, then you must write it.

TONI MORRISON
Nobel Prize-Winning Author

Outside of a dog, a book is man's best friend. Inside a dog, it's too dark to read.

GROUCHO MARX

All good books have one thing in common—they are truer than if they had really happened, and after you have read one of them, you will feel all that happened, happened to you and then it belongs to you forever: the happiness and unhappiness, good and evil, ecstasy and sorrow, the food, wine, beds, people and the weather. If you can give that to the readers, then you're a writer.

ERNEST HEMINGWAY

Dedicated to Writers Everywhere

**Keep the Faith,
You Will Be Published**

Acknowledgments

Grammar Report evolved from an idea to a book thanks to the assistance of many people. Without them, I could have never completed it.

Thanks are extended to John Cangany, a gifted student with an expertise in English literature and an eye for good writing, and Christina Williams, a superb poet and expert in the field who has influenced many with her teaching abilities.

Contributing Editor Heidi Newman is a valued colleague who has assisted many Books For Life Foundation clients. She works tirelessly to eradicate typos and polish text . She is also a strong advocate for aspiring authors and poets.

Thanks to Sara Charette for her layout of the book. Her editing skills are also appreciated. And to Nancy Crenshaw for her valuable assistance with the editing process.

Marie Butler-Knight, publisher of Alpha Books, an imprint of Penguin Group USA, literary agent Kimberly Cameron, former Simon and Schuster senior editor Paul McCarthy, former publisher Kent Carroll, author Jodee Blanco, and screenwriter Patrick Hasburgh are thanked for being advisors to the Foundation.

I thank Jack Lupton, the founding benefactor of Books For Life Foundation, for his encouragement and friendship. He is a man of few words with a true passion for one of them. His sidekick Audrey is a saint, and his business guru Dave Gonzenbach is a treasured supporter of the foundation.

The support of my brother Jack, and sisters Anne and Debbie is most appreciated. I know my mother and father are guiding me from Heaven.

Thanks are also offered to my canine pal, Black Sox. His companionship at five a.m. is heartwarming.

Above all, I thank the Good Lord for blessing me with the creativity and dedication necessary to become an author. Without His guidance, I am nothing.

Mark Shaw
Author

Contents

Author's Note

Correct grammar and punctuation usage are essential for all writers, but both are critical for aspiring authors and poets with dreams of becoming traditionally published. No matter how terrific the book idea is, or how marketable it may be, grammar and punctuation mistakes restrict serious consideration by literary agents and publishers.

Relax - no one is asking you to become a proofreader or grammar specialist. Help can be garnered from experienced line editors, but it is essential that you create clean, clear, and credible work prior to having an editor peruse your material.

While reading this book, remember that the suggestions and tips included are based on accepted guidelines, not hard and fast rules. Even the experts sometimes disagree about grammar and punctuation issues, and writers should adhere to a consensus of opinion regarding proper usage.

To be certain, *Grammar Report* is not an authoritative guide crafted by a writing instructor or leading expert in the field. Advice is presented in a practical, "what you need to know" format based on my experiences as a published author, and more important, consultation with many writers through Books For Life Foundation, the not-for-profit organization we created to educate authors and poets about the publishing process.

After reading countless manuscripts, poetry collections, magazine and newspaper articles, short stories, essays, book proposals, and query letters, I began recognizing a common thread to writing woes. To my surprise, mistakes were quite fundamental, and repeated by writers unfamiliar, either through lack of education or due to inactivity since their school days, with the basics of English usage rules. While reviewing written materials, I noted common errors committed by those with publishing aspirations. Knowing that such mistakes would be costly during submission to literary agents or publishers, I decided a short-form book focusing on the basics of good grammar and punctuation was essential.

As a supplement to *Book Report: Publishing Strategies, Writing Tips, and 101 Literary Ideas For Aspiring Authors and Poets,* and *Poetry Report, Creative Ideas and Publishing Strategies For Aspiring Poets, Grammar Report* is intended for those specifically interested in becoming traditionally published. In addition, my hope is that the content will be beneficial to everyday writers—those who pen journal entries, business letters, and even personal letters to friends and family. Written words are special, a communication from one heart to another, and thus the text must be free of common grammar and punctuation mistakes. During seminars on writing and publishing alternatives sponsored by Books For Life Foundation, I like to use the expression, "You are what you write." If you agree, I trust you want your work to be the best it can be. *Grammar Report* will aid you in this effort.

This book, written through a collaborative effort with editing guru Heidi Newman and poet Christina Williams, is divided into five sections and an Appendix. "Grammar Grabbers" and "Punctuation Points" focus on grammar usage and provide practical information. Realizing writers' attention spans are shorter than the time it takes for a dog to decide to chase a rabbit, the sections feature information in quick-reference format. If you only grasp half of the grammar and punctuation principles outlined in "Grammar Grabbers" and "Punctuation Points," you will at least improve your writing to the point where it is not infiltrated with embarrassing mistakes. Lists of commonly misspelled words and words confused for one another are also included as a reference.

Aspiring poets can discover inspiration in "Poetry Punctuation and Grammar," a section devoted to understanding proper form. Poetry is a different animal from other forms of writing, but Christina Williams and I have paid special attention to practical advice that will assist beginners who wonder what poetry grammar or punctuation standard is expected.

Section Four presents Writing for Publication, an area that focuses on word usage and more. In *Book Report*, I stated, "There is not a *right* word to use, but there is a *best* word." Since words are the writer's tool to communicate with readers, choices that move the story along, offer description or sentiment, quicken the pace, and increase the drama are paramount. This section begins with a few reminders regarding the basics: nouns, verbs, adverbs, adjectives, and agreement. If you have not studied English for some time, a visit to "Writing For Publication" before reading the other sections may be advisable.

To enable writers to discover immediate assistance regarding proper grammar and punctuation usage, a "question and answer" format is utilized. Examples are provided to enhance the solutions. Where required, alternatives are presented. A reference source is noted when it is advisable for authors and poets to conduct further research about the specific writing challenge facing them.

I trust this book will also be beneficial to experienced writers who may need to brush up on their grammar and punctuation. Sources besides *Grammar Report* include *Elements of Style* by William Strunk, Jr. and E. B. White and the *Chicago Manual of Style*. The latter appears to be the publication most often consulted in the book publishing industry.

To enhance visualization, a "Learning from Others" Appendix is featured at the end of the book. It is suggested that aspiring authors and poets scrutinize text written by best-selling authors and poets to see what makes it sizzle – what makes it classic. Watch closely how vivid the writing is and how proper word choice and proper punctuation trigger a pacing that moves the message along. All writers are storytellers and their words must keep readers turning the pages.

As you read the text, remember that many of the writers violate rules noted in this book. Be certain to learn from the good writing while avoiding the mistakes that even experienced writers make. As far as I can tell, the perfect book has not been written yet and I doubt it will be.

To aid writers interested in longer form text, excerpts from two books are also presented. Remember that good writing is all about providing readers with a good beginning, middle, and end to each sentence, paragraph, and chapter. This leads to terrific storytelling.

To those who are determined to be traditionally published, I caution you to use the grammar and punctuation directives listed in this book and others in tandem with employing a professional editor before text is submitted to literary agents and publishers. Regardless of your level of expertise, a good copyeditor can spot errors, redundancies, inconsistencies and omissions that can destroy good text. Being one's own editor is impossible. Make certain to employ a professional who will be objective with regard to the material. Locating editors is easy – and one of the many consulting services we provide through Books For Life Foundation.

Improving grammar and punctuation takes practice. Supplemented by author Stephen King's advice as to how to become a better writer ("Read a lot, and write a lot"), aspiring authors and poets can self-educate to the point where they are accomplished wordsmiths with exciting stories to tell. Their works will be considered by literary agents and publishers in accordance with query letter and book proposal components outlined in *Book Report*, *Poetry Report,* and the BFLF software program, My Book Proposal. This will not guarantee the writer a publishing contract, but it will guarantee the material they submit will be considered on its merits, and not discarded for lack of proper form or because it is infested with grammatical and punctuation mistakes.

This said, enjoy *Grammar Report*. Read, make notes (the author welcomes ideas to include in the next edition), and learn. And Godspeed to you as a writer — with a terrific book idea, hard work, and perseverance, you ***will*** be published!

Mark Shaw

Grammar Grabbers

Grammar Grabbers

Imagine you are a literary agent or an editor at a publishing company. Upon returning from one of those famous New York three-hour lunches at a fancy restaurant, you sit behind a desk and stare at the three-foot-tall stack of query letters and book proposals your assistant has delivered. Before she did so, **any manuscripts received from unpublished authors or poets have been thrown in the trash bin since you do not have time to read a four-hundred-page novel or a fifty-page collection of poetry.**

Armed with a full tummy of sushi and hot sake, you begin to scan the query letters and book proposals. You are impressed that these aspiring authors and poets have done their homework by checking the guidelines presented in *Book Report; Poetry Report; The Guide to Literary Agents; Writer's Market; Poet's Market; Children's Writer's and Illustrator's Market,* and other credible self-help books that are a writer's best friends.

Selecting one book proposal with the title, *The Day the Earth Moved*, you begin to read the accompanying query letter. Per your guidelines and industry standards, it is one page in length, single-spaced. **Immediately, the first line grabs your attention since it presents a "what-if" scenario.** Your emotions stir as you think, "Hey, maybe this is just the novel I have been looking for," but then your face reddens as you notice several glaring grammatical errors. First, the author has used "there" where it should be "their," and next "I" where it should be "me."

Pressed for time, your glee in discovering a good "what-if" scenario dissipates, and you toss the query letter and proposal into the bin marked "Return to Sender." This writers' graveyard is the dead end for aspiring authors or poets since they have not been judged on the merit of the book idea, but disqualified because of grammatical errors.

To ensure query letters and book proposals will be considered on their merits, make certain the text is error-free. To aid your effort, listed below are fifty quick tips designed to provide a working knowledge of proper grammar usage. Presented in a question-and-answer format, they are designed to aid your efforts in submitting a mistake-free book idea to interested agents and publishers. You have thus optimized your opportunity to become published – the ultimate goal of any aspiring writer.

---

1. Stephen King said, "The adverb is not your friend." What did he mean?

King and many other writing experts believe that if you have to use an adverb to assist the meaning of the verb, use another verb. Before submitting text, whether it is a query letter, a book proposal, or any manuscript, consider adverb surgery. Eliminate as many as possible. This impresses readers since it says to them that you understand good word usage and don't need a crutch to lean on.

Examples:
The cat raced quickly to avoid the oncoming dump truck. (no)
The cat raced to avoid the oncoming dump truck. (yes)
Alex thoroughly searched for the missing paper clips. (no)
Alex searched two hours for the missing paper clips. (yes)
Polly was really excited to receive the award. (no)

2. Does Stephen King hate adjectives as well? Don't adjectives add flavor?

Once in a while, yes; every other word, no. Nouns are precious commodities. They are the foundation for sentences and should be explosive. As pillars of text, they must stand alone without the need for a fancy friend whose purpose is to tell you how great the noun is. Instead, search for nouns that leap off the page into readers' brains. Inspect your writing to discover if you present the best ones possible. Don't forget that when a query letter, a book proposal, a manuscript, or a collection of poetry is being read, it is tantamount to your having a conversation with the reader, but you are not there. To ensure your writing is visual, uncover the best noun available and you will clip unnecessary adjectives from the text.

Examples:
The flashy, self-absorbed, spent-looking woman entered the seedy brothel. (no)
The loquacious madam sauntered into the brothel. (yes)
Wilbur attended the race with his perky, fun-loving, cheerful sister. (no)
Wilbur attended the race with his gregarious sister. (yes)

3. What is wrong with using clichés?

Those who live by the cliché die by the cliché. This "hybrid cliché" suggests that those writers who rely on overused phrases signal their inability to create fresh words to provide description. Whether it is a query letter or book proposal outlining non-fiction, fiction or verses of poetry, a collection of short stories, an essay, or a novel or non-fiction manuscript, don't fall into the "cliché trap." Show (don't tell) readers you possess a vivid imagination and are a professional who takes the time to find the best words to trigger emotion, information, or inspiration.

Examples:
Charles rolled with the punches when Stan berated his behavior. (no)
He was the cat's meow when he hit the dance floor. (no)
Sally was concerned about Dan when he talked of his pie-in-the-sky dreams. (no)
Dan likened Alice's eyes to the color of sycamore leaves. (yes)
Carl decided Rex was meaner than a dog whose tail had been stepped on. (yes)

4. I love using metaphors and similes. What's wrong with them?

Metaphor, like simile, can be the author's or poet's friend, as long as it is not too close a friend. Use of multiple metaphors to compare two seemingly different concepts overwhelms readers, leaving them to wonder why the author or poet leans on this lazy crutch when fresh words are available. To impress literary agents and publishers, writers must be unique and present a creative style and use of the language that sets them apart from the multitude of writers submitting material for publishing consideration.

Examples:
Sally ran like the wind to win the race. (no)
Sally sprinted to the lead and never looked back. (yes)
John kept his mouth shut knowing silence is the most powerful message. (yes)

Similes can describe two potentially abstract ideas as well. They can be located by watching for words such as "like" and "as." Be careful not to overuse them.

Examples:
The man in the hat decided he would run like there was no tomorrow. (no)
Peter grabbed the pole like it was his best friend. (yes)
She was as eager as a coon dog on a chase. (yes)
Trip swam like a porpoise in heat. (yes)

5. Is there a general rule for the use of "a" and "an"?

Use "a" before consonant sounds and "an" before vowel sounds. To test your use, say the sentence out loud. Many times you can "feel" what is proper from the tone of the words being spoken.

Examples:
Donna ate a apple a day. (no)
Polly was an only child. (yes)
An orange a day will keep doctor bills to a minimum. (yes)
Prince is an exciting artist and a lover of many varieties of music. (yes)

6. I like to use the word "that" as a descriptive word in my text. Am I being unprofessional?

Writers should conduct "that" searches to locate text locations where the word is not required. It is amazing how many can be eliminated without losing any sense of meaning. Be careful, though: non-use of the word where it is required can be as bad as using it too often.

Examples:
Robert thought that the orchestra was playing a bit flat. (no)
Robert thought the orchestra was playing a bit flat. (yes)
Rex chose to stay, a decision that provided him an opportunity to study art. (no)
Rex chose to stay, a decision providing him an opportunity to study art. (yes)

7. When I have a character speak, do I need to use "he said," or "she said," all the time?

No, you do not, but be careful to be clear about who is speaking. Also – you do not need to use explanations in your verbiage such as "he said emphatically," or "she told him excitedly." Your words should do the talking. If they don't, draft new words.

Examples:
"I'm concerned about Ted," Alice said grumblingly. (no)
"Let's go to the beach!" Wilbur shouted to everyone. (yes)
"Are you going to meet me in the morning?" Silowan asked. (yes)

8. When do I use "important," vs. "importantly"?

There appears to be no consensus of opinion regarding the correct usage. Using "important" may be preferable, but use of "importantly" won't earn you a trip to the grammar doghouse.

Examples:
More importantly, he was an above average student at Duke. (yes)
More important, he was an above average student at Duke. (yes)

9. Whether to use "all right" or "alright" is difficult to know. What is proper?

Actually, purists believe that the proper usage is "all right," but modern times appear to favor the use of "alright." Watch how the word is being used. This can be a deciding factor.

Examples:
Oprah said it was alright for me to kiss Fred. (yes)
My answers on the quiz were all right. (meaning answers were all correct)
My answers on the quiz were alright. (meaning answers were satisfactory)
Richard donned his jacket and said, "Alright, I'm ready to go." (yes)

10. Deciding whether to use "sit" or "set" causes me to break out in hives. What is proper?

General rule: Sit is only used in the context of sitting down. Set is used in the context of positioning or placing something. Keep this rule in mind and you will never go wrong even though people will tell you there is a better rule.

Examples:
"Alex said to Sid, "Set down and talk to me." (no)
Rover decided he had to sit on my lap and drool. (yes)
Oscar set the plates and saucers beside the table. (yes)
Sit down and take a break. (yes)

11. Are "lie" and "lay" interchangeable?

Don't spend much time trying to figure out which of these words, or their derivatives, is proper since you will end up in a mental institution. A common way of thinking about them is to say, "I use 'lay' when I am going to put something somewhere." Otherwise you "lie" as in "I am going to lie down."

Examples:
"Lie the Bible down on the table," Pete said. (no)
"Lie down Abe," Paul said, "or you will be tired for the rest of the day. (yes)
Lay the music by the piano and begin your singing lessons. (yes)
He laid the brick on the doorstep before returning to his car. (yes)
Sylvia was lying in the shade of an oak tree. (yes)

12. Is it proper to write, "Can I cut the grass?"

Use "can" in the context of ability to do something while "may" is used in the context of requesting permission.

Examples:
"Can I have the roast beef sandwich?" Troy asked. (no)
George asked, "May I escort Olivia to the prom?" (yes)
He may go to the store, but we'll wait to see if he can behave himself. (yes)

13. I hear people say "among" and "amongst." Which is correct?

Both forms are considered acceptable, but "among" is the better of the two since it is shorter and more informal. The same thing is true regarding "amid" and "amidst."

Examples:
Don't run amongst the bulls or you will get stomped. (no)
Jonah and Alice were among friends when they entered the pool hall. (yes)
The robbers decided to split the money among the four boys. (yes)
He was stronger amid the rest of the men. (yes)

14. I get the use of "who," who's," and "whose" mixed up. What is appropriate?

When deciding whether to use "who's" or "whose," read aloud the sentence you are contemplating. Since "who's" is the contraction for "who is," you will be able to tell if the two words fit with the meaning of the sentence or whether the use of "whose," a pronoun, will be proper.

Examples:
Who's baseball bat is this and why is it laying here? (no)
The real question he had was, "Who's on first?" (yes)
Johnny was a lonely boy whose father had abandoned him. (yes)
Who's going to the basketball game with Sally and Linda? (yes)

15. When do I use "nor" and when is "or" appropriate?

"Neither/nor" is a tag team to watch for. "Nor" may be proper without "neither," but seldom.

Examples:
Neither Abbott or Costello was in attendance. (no)
Neither Melvin nor Mark was tall. (yes)
Fred cannot speak nor can he hear. (yes)
The young boy was neither bright nor industrious. (yes)

She was not on time, nor was she willing to hurry. (yes)

16. Use of "shall" and "will" confuses me. What is proper?

"Shall" is normally used with first-person writing and "will" with second- and third-person text.

Examples:
Sheila shall run across the yard. (no)
I shall overcome my tendencies to become angry. (yes)
Sylvia will leave the church and become a missionary. (yes)
The umpire will be leaving the game but I shall never forget his ineptness. (yes)

17. The words assure, insure, and ensure drive me batty. What is correct?

If you want to "make sure," use ensure. Assure means you are attempting to tell someone everything will be okay. Stick with insure when you are dealing with insurance matters.

Examples:
He ensured his car for twenty-five thousand dollars. (no)
Colin assured the nation he would not run for president. (yes)
To ensure a stable future, Eric attended Harvard business school. (yes)
I told him to insure the house for $100,000. (yes)

18. "Convince" and "persuade" appear to be interchangeable. Are they?

No. If you are attempting to convince someone, it normally deals with the thought process. On the other hand, persuade involves action; attempting to cause someone to do something.

Examples:
Alexander tried to persuade Solomon he was a saint. (no)
Alexander attempted to convince Solomon he was a saint. (yes)
To persuade him to try out for the debate team, she read him the rules. (yes)

Persuade her to stay and I will bake a raspberry pie. (yes)

19. How can I tell when it is proper to use "among" or "between?"

A good general rule is to use "among" when discussing more than two things or persons unless they are being considered individually.

Examples:
Between the brothers, he was the fastest. (no)
The shortstop position would be decided among four players. (yes)
Why can't you stop bickering among yourselves? (yes)
The debate was between Claude, Helga, and their professor. (yes)

20. I've been criticized for my use of the word "they" when I'm describing action by a character. What is the problem?

Disagreement between nouns and pronouns - mixing singular and plural - is looked upon with disfavor. Be careful not to describe the work of an organization or other entity as "they" when "it" is proper.

Examples:
The Police Athletic League is a terrific organization and they help officers. (no)
Each clown puts on their own makeup. (no)
Each clown puts on his or her own makeup. (yes)
A good writer watches his or her punctuation usage. (yes)
Authors and poets are talented and they deserve applause for their efforts. (yes)

21. I often have trouble deciding whether to use "which" or "that." What is proper?

"Which" is used when adding information about an object already identified. Use of "that" narrows a category or identifies a subject being discussed. "Which" is often preceded by a comma, parentheses or a dash.

Examples:
The shoes which are in the closet are quite comfortable. (yes)
The shoes, which are in the closet, need polishing. (yes)
I heard a song that reminded me of my high school prom. (yes)

22. Should I write in first person, second person, third person, or may I combine them?

Writing in first person means the narrator is participating in the action. Writing in second person is normally restricted to instructional books when the author speaks directly to readers. Writing in third person permits the narrator to observe the action. Any of these written communications is proper, but do not mix them without careful thought.

Examples:
(1st person) From behind the haystack, I watched the enemy soldiers.
(2nd person) When you decide to write, make sure you use proper grammar.
(3rd person) Frederick avoided the stare of the lovely woman and walked away.

23. I'm confused about tenses. How do I decide what would be most interesting to the reader?

Text may be written in present, past or future tense. Present tense involves action taking place currently. Past tense deals with action that has already occurred. Future tense is action that will happen. The key is not to confuse readers by mixing them.

Examples:
Lenore called her on the telephone and she picks it up on the third ring. (no)
Lenore called her on the telephone and she picked it up on the third ring. (yes)
Frankie was an addict and his drug of choice is speed. (no)
Frankie was an addict and his choice of drug was speed. (yes)
I will call my mom because I was going to tell her a secret. (no)
I will call my mom and tell her a secret. (yes)

24. Is it permissible to use "But" or "And" at the start of a sentence?

There is a difference of opinion regarding its use, but it is proper. Be careful not to overuse this word choice or to present a fragmented sentence.

Examples:
Pam ran to the store. But before the rain fell. (no - fragment)
Pam ran to the store, but before the rain fell. (yes)
Art practiced diving in the lap pool. But he left before the competition. (yes)
The truth was apparent to Tom. But recent developments left him puzzled. (yes)
Johnny saw the cat. And then turned around when he heard a hiss. (yes)

25. When is it proper to use the word "etc." to indicate more is intended?

"Etc." means there are more examples or there is something more the subject said, but you are not going to provide that information. Avoid if possible, and instead use "including," or "such as."

Examples:
Paul was left with many choices, etc. etc. etc. (no)
The rain was accompanied by lightning, thunder, hail, etc. (no)
Jim wondered if Arnie was angry, anxious, or just grouchy. (yes)
Pat packed many items such as raincoats, socks, boots, and hats. (yes)

26. Deciding when to use "further" and "farther" causes me severe headaches. What is the distinction?

When designating distance, use "farther." "Further" is best used to denote quantities or abstract concepts or notions.

Examples:
James was further from the goal than Pistol Pete. (no)
Suspicious, Owen decided to look into the matter further. (yes)
Jupiter is farther from the earth than the moon. (yes)
The farther the golf ball traveled, the less it stayed in bounds. (yes)

27. Is it wrong to use "however" in my writing?

Words such as "however," "nevertheless," and "fortunately" are overused. I call these words "interrupt words" because writers often use them as filler.

Examples:
Johnnie ran to the cleaners, however, he was late. (no)
Johnnie ran to the cleaners. He was late. (yes)
Fortunately, Rex loved Debbie for her looks not her money. (no)
Rex loved Debbie for her looks and not her money. (yes)

28. Is there such a word as "irregardless?"

No. The proper word is "regardless."

Examples:
Irregardless of the weather, he paddled in the surf. (no)
Regardless of the outcome, the championship fight was a success. (yes)
The teacher liked John regardless of his tendency to be late for class. (yes)

29. "Is it proper to use "as per" in a sentence?

It is only proper if you don't ever want to write anything professionally in your life. Always use "per."

Examples:
As per your instructions, I will be leaving the fort at five o'clock. (no)
Per your instructions, I will be leaving the fort at five o'clock. (yes)
John decided to attend the soccer game per the note in his locker. (yes)

30. I'm a lover of the words "very" and "really." Is it okay to use them for emphasis?

"Very" and "really" are unnecessary most of the time. Use strong, visual words and they can stand alone.

Examples:
Sal was very interested in becoming a professor at the university. (no)
Sal was committed to becoming a professor at the university. (yes)
Steve was so interested in becoming tenured he made a pact with the devil. (yes)

31. How do I know whether to use "him" or "he?"

Reading the text out loud assists your choice. To test usage, try replacing "him" with "me," and see if the sentence flows. For example, in the following sentence, "Paula danced with him and his brother," replacing "him" with "me" fits. But "Paula danced with I and his brother sounds incorrect, so "he" is not the right choice. If the action is performed *by* the subject, use subjective pronouns I, he, she, or they. If the action is done *to* the subject, use objective pronouns, me, him/her, or them.

Examples:
Charlie left with he and Margaret for the movies. (no)
I wanted to know him better before we dated. (yes)
After all, it was he who called to see if I was feeling better. (yes)
If the choice is clear, Alex will be with him and not Rex. (yes)

32. What about use of "her" or "she?"

Use the same rules as above. Speak the words and see what fits. Test your usage by leaving out one subject. The pronoun should stand alone. In the final example, if you left out "Marlene," it would only sound correct to say "Tony asked her," not "Tony asked she."

Examples:
Bob took Sheila and she to the movies. (no)
Bob took Sheila and her to the movies. (yes)
I left she at the gate, and traveled the distance on foot. (no)
I left her at the gate, and traveled the distance on foot. (yes)
Tony asked her and Marlene for the truth. (yes)

33. When to use "who" and "whom" is a tough decision. What are my options?

A good general rule to remember: Use "whom" when denoting the recipient and not the subject of the action. To test usage, replace "whom" with "him" and "he." If "he" sounds better, use "who." If "him" sounds better, use "whom."

Examples:
To who am I am speaking? (no)
To whom am I speaking? (yes)
Fred, whom is calling me? (no)
Fred, who is calling me? (yes)
Lucy, who is the head cook, brought me a piece of cake. (yes)

34. Use of "I" or "me" in a sentence is confusing. Is there a set standard?

Usually "I" denotes the one in action while "me" is the object of an action. If there are two subjects or objects of the action, test usage by leaving out one subject to see what sounds right on its own.

Examples:
Claudia loves Sharon and I. (no) [Claudia loves me.]
Alfred and me attended the opera opening. (no) [I attended the opera…]
Abe called out to Sid and me. (yes)
["Abe called out to I" sounds wrong. "Me" in the above sentence is correct.]

35. Whether to use "one another" or "each other" drives me crazy. How can I decide what is correct?

Your sanity is saved. The term "each other" refers to two people while "one another" is used to denote three or more people. Enough said.

Examples:
The five boys and I said to each other, "should we go fishing?" (no)
The three girls hung around one another like they were sisters. (yes)
"We love each other," John said to Arlene. (yes)
Why don't you and Fred and the twins see one another in September. (yes)

36. Is bestseller one word or two? How about the same question for such words as work week, schoolyear, and website?

Internet spell-checks can be helpful, but the dictionary is a remarkable resource. If you can't find a word in the dictionary, ask an editor or proofreader.

Examples:
The book was a bestseller on the *New York Times* list. (preferred)
He endured a sixty-hour workweek. (yes)
The school year lasted two hundred sixty days. (yes)
Dorothy worked online to prepare her thesis. (preferred)

37. I like to use abbreviations in my text. Is this alright?

Our fast-food society has adopted coined terms to describe nearly every aspect of life. We thus say paper instead of newspaper, photo instead of photograph, and worse than worse, phone instead of telephone. While this is acceptable if you are using a colloquial voice, professional authors and poets using the formal voice do not accede to this lazy way of writing. Instead they use the proper word in their text. This is impressive to literary agents and publishers who value the written word.

Examples:

Improper:	**Proper:**
TV	Television
Ad	Advertisement

38. Does the above information apply to use of names like doctor, lieutenant, mister, and reverend?

Abbreviations are proper for certain designations like those stated above unless they are used before a name in direct quotations.

Examples:
Flashbulbs blinded Doctor Lind as he walked up the courthouse steps. (no)
Flashbulbs blinded Dr. Lind as he walked up the courthouse steps. (yes)
Lt. Johnson carried himself well. (yes)

The lieutenant walked with a limp. (yes)
He loved the play, "Doctor Doolittle." (yes)

39. When do I use "who" or "that" when describing the actions of a character?

Use "who" when you are dealing with humans and "that" otherwise. This rule should pull you through.

Examples:
There was a story by a newspaper reporter that loved the written word. (no)
There was a story by a newspaper reporter who loved the written word. (yes)
The corporation executives who stole the money should be in prison. (yes)

40. I write sentence fragments. Is there an easy way to fix them?

I'm pleased you asked. To effectively turn dastardly fragments into complete sentences, writers should understand that there are two types of clauses combined to create different types of sentences. First, there is the independent clause, the subject and predicate structure that forms the backbone of sentences. They include a noun and a verb. The clause is "independent" since it can stand on its own. A dependent clause that does not contain the noun/verb pairing cannot stand alone.

Examples:
Because Claude had no money. (no).
Because he had no money, Claude left the store. (yes)
Peter brought them tissues, they were sneezing. (no)
Peter brought them tissues because they were sneezing. (yes)

41. All of the sentences I write look the same. How can I vary the structure?

To vary the sentence structure, try using simple sentences, compound sentences, complex sentences, and compound-complex sentences. Each sentence utilizes different combinations of independent and dependent clauses.

Examples:
Simple: Antonio Banderas walked to the movie set.
Compound: Antonio Banderas drove to the movie and ran into a mailbox.
Complex: Antonio Banderas walked the dog before it rained.
Compound-Complex: Before it rained, Antonio Banderas walked to the movie set and was joined by his wife and pet chicken.

42. When there are mistakes in a quote I am using, should I correct them?
Regardless of the text, a quote should be repeated accurately. If you are quoting someone from an interview you have conducted and wish to alter the wording for grammatical purposes so the person will not be embarrassed, you must receive the interviewee's permission. If you decide to use part of the quoted material, and feel that doing so might be objectionable, consult with him or her.

Examples:
Hugh told me, "Golf is a young man's sport and they love it." (no)
Hugh told me, "Golf is a young man's sport and he loves it." (yes)
Frederick said, "I never seen anyone prettier than her." (yes – direct quote)

43. I'm dumbfounded regarding when to capitalize "Dad," "Father," "Mom" and "Mother," and when to not do so.

Relax your worried mind. Remember – capitalize when used as proper noun or title. Always use lower case when using "my," "him, or "her."

Examples:
I love my Mother more than anyone. (no)
After the film, Mom and I wept. (yes)
I love my mother more than anything. (yes)
My dad and I decided to shop in the mall. (yes)
He saw Fred's mother walking to the market. (yes)
Dad, watch out! (yes)

44. Are "ask" and "asked" interchangeable?

No, they are not and if you mix them up, membership in the Grammar Society of America is forsaken. "Ask" is a present tense word while "asked' deals with past tense. Watch usage since this is a telltale sign of unprofessional conduct for a writer who does not do his homework.

Examples:
I asked you, "Does he understand what I am saying?" (no)
I ask you, "Does he understand what I am saying?" (yes)
The preacher has ask that you parishioners quiet down during prayer. (no)
The preacher has asked that you parishioners quiet down during prayer. (yes)

45. Is it proper to say Mr. and Mrs. Sally Anne Barker?

No, you have created Mr. Sally Barker. He will object to this.

Examples:
The president intends to invite Mr. and Mrs. John Barker. (yes)

Mrs. Sally Ann Baker is married to John. (yes)
Where is the invitation for the Canganys, John and Alice? (yes)

46. Is it alright to use the words "the fact that"?

Curse the day you do so. Edit them out since there are other words that will accomplish your intended mission.

Examples:
The fact is that he was an awful man and I'm pleased he failed. (no)
He was an awful man and I'm pleased he failed. (yes)
In spite of the fact that Aubrey drank whiskey every day, he was okay. (no)
Aubrey drank whiskey every day, but he was okay. (yes)

47. I like to use contractions since they are more conversational. What is proper?

Scattered use is acceptable, but don't overuse contractions. Read your words out loud to see if a contraction is really required.

Examples:
They'd be better off dead. (Better – They would be better off dead.)
I have never seen a woman like Rosy. (yes)
Who would have ever believed he'd be a famous ballplayer? (yes)

48. I confuse use of "because" and "since." Is there an easy way to tell when to use them?

Grammatically, there is no real difference between "because" and "since," but "since" is used to relay a sense of time while "because" is used with a cause/effect relationship.

Examples:
Because she was born, Sally has loved to play in the yard with the dog. (no)
Since she lost her hearing, Sally has loved to play in the yard with the dog. (yes)

Because I left the opera early, I missed the finale. (yes)
Since the last time I saw Clem, I fell in love with Rex. (yes)

49. Is there a handy-dandy rule to follow regarding subject and pronoun agreement?

Don't use "their" when the subject is singular. Pronouns such as everybody, everyone, either, neither, somebody and anyone may sound plural, but they are usually treated as singular, and require singular corresponding pronouns and verbs.

Examples:
Each writer wanted their books back. (no)
He and she wanted their books back. (yes)
Each writer wanted his or her book back. (yes: each is singular)

Everyone wants to be noticed for their academic achievements. (no)
Everyone wants to be noticed for his or her academic achievements. (yes)
It's great to have a dog like Black Sox who entertains themselves. (no)
It's great to have a dog like Black Sox who entertains himself. (yes)

50. I know misspellings are careless and confusing one word for another is a no-no, but are there tips you can give me to spot common mistakes in this area?

Pleased you asked! Computer spell-check is good for catching some misspellings, but not for finding incorrect words used. Here are lists of commonly misspelled words as well as those that appear to be misused on a regular basis:

List of commonly misspelled words:

Correct Spelling	Frequently Misspelled As:
accidentally	accidently
acknowledgment	acknowledgement
a lot	alot
desperate	desparate
development	developement

Correct Spelling	Frequently Misspelled As:
embarrass	embarass
harassment	harrassment
independent	independant
indispensable	indispensible
irresistible	irresistable
irritable	irritible
memento	momento

millennium	millenium
privilege	privelige
repetition	repitition
sacrilegious	sacreligious
seize	sieze
separate	seperate
yield	yield

Notes:

Homonyms, Homophones, and Other Confusing Words:

Note: These words sound alike or look similar, but they can have vastly differing meanings. If you aren't certain which the correct one is, become familiar with their meanings and spellings. Even the best spellers can slip up and use the wrong word because it "sounds" right. But using the wrong word causes readers to stumble, making the writer look careless or lazy – or unintelligent.

accept, except

Notes:

ad, add

affect, effect

aid, aide, ade

air, heir, err

altar, alter

any way, anyway

backyard, back yard

bare, bear

born, borne

break, brake

burned, burnt

buy, by, bye

carat, carrot, caret, karat

cent, scent, sent

cite, site, sight

Notes:

compliment, complement

core, corps

counsel, council

course, coarse

dammed, damned

depend, deepened, deep end

die, dye

discrete, discreet

elicit, illicit

everyday, every day

fair, fare

faze, phase

feat, feet

flare, flair

flour, flower

for, fore, four

forth, fourth

forward, foreword

gorilla, guerilla

hale, hail

hangar, hanger

hay, hey

hear, here

heroin, heroine

incite, insight

inquire, enquire

its, it's

lead, led

lessen, lesson

lightning, lightening

loan, lone

loose, lose

manner, manor

marry, merry

meat, meet, mete

medal, meddle

metal, mettle

moose, mousse

naval, navel

one, won

pair, pare, pear

palate, pallet, palette

passed, past

peace, piece

prays, preys, praise

principal, principle

profit, prophet

Notes:

rain, rein, reign

raise, raze, rays

real, reel

recreate, re-create

regimen, regiment

right, rite, write

road, rode, rowed

root, route

rye, wry

savor, saver

seam, seem

shear, sheer

slight, sleight

so, sew, sow

sole, soul

sore, soar

spade, spayed

stake, steak

stationary, stationery

steal, steel

sweet, suite

tail, tale

taut, taught

team, teem

Notes:

teas, tease, tees

then, than

they're, there, their

threw, through

tic, tick

to, too, two

toad, towed, toed

tracked, tract

vain, vein

vary, very

verses, versus

vice, vise

ware, where, wear

waste, waist

weather, whether

whale, wail

whined, wined, wind

whole, hole

whose, who's

won't, wont

yoke, yolk

Notes:

Punctuation Points

Punctuation Points

The sentence, “‘“I see beautiful stars in the sky”, Alice commented’”. is a killer for any aspiring author or poet. By inserting the comma and the period *after* the quotation marks and by not knowing how to properly use quotation marks, the writer has shouted to the literary world, “I am a novice whose work is not worthy of serious consideration.”

Correct punctuation is an essential tool for the writer, a thumbprint regarding his or her professionalism. Punctuation mistakes are red flags that stop the reading process.

As stated in the Author’s Note, any serious writer aspiring to publish should hire a professional line editor or copyeditor to scan his or her material prior to submission, but before doing so, work hard to eliminate punctuation errors. This will permit the editor to better evaluate the content. It will also reduce the amount of proofreading expense incurred by the writer.

Below are twenty-six essential tips to aid the effort.

---

1. I have trouble deciding whether punctuation marks are located inside or outside quotation marks. What is the general rule?

The general rule is that commas and periods are located inside quotation marks. Semi-colons and colons are normally positioned outside the quotation marks. When the entire sentence is a question or exclamation, the question mark or exclamation point is located outside the quotation mark. If the entire sentence is a question, the question mark is located outside the quotation mark. When only the quoted material is a question or exclamation, the question mark or exclamation point is inside the quotation mark.

Examples:

“Was Rex correct when he answered, “Brazil?” (no)
“Was Rex correct when he answered, “Brazil”? (yes)
“*Annie Hall* is my favorite film”, Woody Allen said. (no)
“*Annie Hall* is my favorite film,” Woody Allen said. (yes)
Olivia screamed, “I love you Brad!” (yes)
Axel hated the phrase, “Be all you can be”; why, we didn’t know. (yes)

2. When is the use of single quotation marks acceptable?

Single quotes are used to signify a quotation within a quotation. They can also be used around unusual or foreign words. Be sure to include the final single quote mark inside the double quotation marks.

Examples:
Paul said to Felix, "I used the words I'm back from the *Terminator*." (no)
Paul said to Felix, "I used the words 'I'm back' from the *Terminator*." (yes)
Osgood began his speech with the words, "My favorite saying is, 'Ain't life grand?'" (yes)
"There is a line in a poem," John said, "that reads 'all love is hate in disguise.'" (yes)
Pete told me to avoid the 'varmit' who fixes trucks with used parts. (yes)

3. When to italicize, when to underline, and when to use quotation marks is a perplexing problem. How can I decide?

Writers should italicize the names of films, books, screenplays, operas, plays, television series, and magazines. Quotation marks are used for book chapters, poems, articles, songs, and short stories. By current publishing standards, underlining for any reason is incorrect. Some writing experts believe that the title of a book not yet published should be in all capital letters. This is optional.

Examples:
Pete and Martin left the movie, A Few Good Men, with haste. (no)
I read MOBY DICK from cover to cover. (no)
Claude and Elizabeth enjoyed *A Beautiful Mind*. (yes)
His poem, "The Artful American," won the festival award. (yes)
My favorite song is Roy Orbison's, "Runnin' Scared." (yes)

4. When I include numbers in my writing, how can I tell whether to use numerical symbols or write the words out?

This varies from publisher to publisher, and there are exceptions, but the general rule is for numbers from zero to ninety-nine, use words; for 100 and above, use the numerical symbol. One more rule: Never start a sentence using the numerical symbol.

Examples:
10 girls kissed the boy's rosy cheek. (no)
Ten girls kissed the boy's rosy cheek. (yes)
Oliver left me twenty stories to edit. (yes)
Frederick won 2 million dollars. (yes)
Alfred won 4 percent of the vote. (yes)
Jerry raced 59 miles to meet her. (yes)
Judy changed the 100-watt light bulb for the second time. (yes)

5. How about when numbers are used to denote age?

There are conflicting opinions regarding whether to spell out numbers or use the numeral symbol. Consistency is more important than which rule is followed.

Examples:
Ralphie turned twenty-five years old last Saturday. (no)
The zoo featured a fifteen-year-old Panda. (no)
The zoo featured a 15-year-old Panda. (yes)

6. When should I use brackets in my sentences?

Tough call at times, but brackets are used sparingly to note an explanation or clarification and not simply more information. Use brackets to further offset information within parentheses or to indicate a missing word.

Examples:
Theodore was the image of his father [now deceased], but better looking. (yes)
(To elaborate on the discussion [of December 3], see the professor.) (yes)
Johnson stated his opinion [of] the amendment in the newspaper. (yes)

7. When should I use parentheses in my writings?

Parentheses provide clarification or additional information about words being used. Do not use them too often, especially in the same sentence, or where commas would suffice.

Examples:
Tickets will be available (at a discounted rate) after dinner. (yes)
The alley cat (a mixed-breed) loved tuna. (yes)
When Freddie danced with Ruth (she was a foot shorter), he hunched over. (yes)

8. What words are capitalized?

A good general rule is that only sentence beginnings and proper nouns are capitalized. Watch capitalizing terms following a colon unless what follows is a proper noun or a complete sentence.

Examples:
The coach set the following goals: win twenty games and the conference. (yes)
The Summers family posted the menu: Turkey and dressing will be served. (yes)
He listed the suspects in order: Polly, Dave, Sue, and Leonard. (yes)
The lineup for today's ballgame includes: shortstop, Mike, and pitcher, Ted. (yes)

9. Whether to use commas, and how many to use, drives me crazy. What is the scoop?

The serial comma (the final comma in a list, usually before the words "and" or "or") is being phased out of use. However, include the serial comma in case of ambiguity or for clearer meaning, such as if the last element is two like items separated by "and."

Examples:
We gathered sticks, rocks, twigs, and bark. (no)

We gathered sticks, rocks, twigs and bark. (yes)
She asked whether we were interested in going to the movie, going dancing, spending time at the lake that evening or resting until tomorrow's trip to the amusement park. (yes)
Books, uniforms, notepads, and pens and pencils were all supplied. (yes)
She wanted to know if I preferred washing, drying, or putting away the dishes. (yes)

10. I've never understood the use of hyphens and dashes. Why is this so confusing?

It isn't. Hyphens are versatile tools since they can be used for many different functions. Single hyphens can join two or more words that serve as a compound adjective *before* the noun they are modifying. If they appear after the noun, no hyphen is required. Double hyphens, or dashes, are used to emphasize certain parts of a sentence or to permit a break in the sentence. They also separate complete thoughts.

Examples:
Jonathan was born into a society considered low class. (yes)
Jonathan was born into a low-class society. (yes)
John Dillinger is a well known criminal. (no)
A well-known criminal is John Dillinger. (yes)
Sylvia leased a house in Italy—somewhere in Tuscany—for the summer. (yes)
There were twenty-nine cats entered in the competition. (yes)

11. Semi-colons should be banished from the English language. Is there a need for them?

The function of a semi-colon is similar to that of the dash, but the semi-colon can also be used with conjunctive adverbs (however, therefore, nevertheless) to introduce a new thought. Short sentences do not necessarily need semi-colons. Instead, commas may be appropriate. Use semi-colons in lists, especially of phrases.

Examples:
Ollie loved Sylvia; but she did not know it. (no)
We tried to drive to Oregon; however, steep mountains blocked our path. (yes)
Ethel and Ricky watched the sky; the stars were glimmering in the night. (yes)
Wanda ordered tuna on rye a pickle spear; potato wedges with cheese, four apple turnovers, and a large coffee, all to go. (yes)

12. Is a comma required before the beginning of a quote in a sentence?

A full-sentence quote should be introduced by a comma, but partial quotes and entertainment titles (books, television, plays, film) don't require a comma to introduce them.

Examples:
Pat recognized the play, *Of Mice and Men*, as a classic. (no)
Humphrey Bogart said, "Here's looking at you kid." (yes)
The author titled his play "To Love or Not to Love." (yes)
Oscar wrote the book "Ugly Men Love Olivia." (yes)

13. Deciding whether I need a comma to separate clauses in a sentence is difficult. Is there a general rule to follow?

If there are subjects in both clauses, separate the clauses with a comma. If there are not, do not use the comma.

Examples:
Paulie glanced in the girls' locker room, but didn't see any naked girls. (no)
Scott glanced in the girl's locker room and didn't see any naked girls. (yes)
Sheila watched the stars, but Pete watched her. (yes)
Claude rounded the bend and headed for home plate. (yes)
Mary washed dishes in the cramped kitchen, and Bob cleared the table. (yes)

14. How can I tell if I have written a "run-on" sentence?

This occurs when the writer uses a comma where a period would be appropriate. Avoid writing long sentences when breaking them up would provide more clarity.

Examples:
John went to the bathroom and then walked into the living room and then left for the movie before he went to see Claudia about their exam grades. (no)
There was a smell in the air of burnt toast and he loved that smell. (no)
Pete loved Alicia. He also loved Cathy and Julie. (yes)
Art was a fan of Sammy Sosa; he watched Cubs games all the time. (yes)

15. When is the use of a long dash (called an em dash) appropriate?

Use of a long dash indicates there is a break in the sentence. In *Elements of Style*, the dash is defined as "a mark of separation stronger than a comma, less formal than a colon, and more relaxed than parentheses."

Examples:
Paulie was a cool guy—and lived in Las Vegas in the winter. (no)
Paulie was a cool guy. He lived in Las Vegas in the winter. (yes)
Sally wanted to teach him a lesson—that he better not mess with her. (yes)
The principal stood out—in the minds of many—because he always wore white socks. (yes)

Note: Em dashes (roughly the width of an 'm', and different from an en dash or hyphen in its look and usage), are symbols that aren't on a standard keyboard but are available in word processing software either as a key command or symbol to be inserted. If you're not sure how to insert them, use two hyphens with no spaces between words or hyphens.

Examples:
She waited—and waited—for the bus.
She waited--and waited--for the bus.

16. Is the first word of a quote capitalized?

Doing so is dependent on how the quote is introduced. Complete phrases require capitalization, but partial quotes may not.

Examples:
The jury foreman stated, "That they live up the street." (no)
The jury foreman stated, "We find the defendant guilty as charged." (yes)
Eleanor explained Ruth's behavior by saying "she's just not herself." (yes)

17. I am mixed up about apostrophes and single quotation marks and sometimes my computer is too. What's the story?

There is a difference between an apostrophe and a single quotation mark. Your computer will often automatically insert the wrong one. An apostrophe is in the shape of a '9' and an open quote mark is in the shape of a '6'. You might have to manually insert the correct symbol and override your word processing software. Remember, an apostrophe is used to show possession (Sheila's dog, the school's gym, all four tires' tread), and in contractions or where letters or numbers are missing (don't read, where's my car, I'm here, '44 was a good year).

Examples:
She screamed, "There is a 'Cadillac-size' cockroach in the cabinet." (yes)
I don't want any 'cause they're stale. (no)
I don't want any 'cause they're stale. (yes)
She grew up in the '70s. (no)
She grew up in the '70s. (yes)

18. Apostrophe rules are confusing. What is acceptable?

Apostrophes are used to form possessives of proper and common nouns, but not pronouns. When a contraction is used, the apostrophe will designate what has been eliminated. Apostrophes are occasionally used to designate plurals of letters such as "abc's" or "the three r's" for clarity." Never add apostrophes to make a noun plural.

Examples:
Sammy ran after the lost dog's. (no)
Don't leave me home with Sally. (yes)
Peter was a 1960s kind of guy. (yes)
Peter was a '60s kind of guy. (yes)
Bob Clark's vacation home is splendid. (yes)
The Clarks' vacation home is splendid. (yes)

19. Use of "it's" or "its" bugs me. Does it make a difference?

"It's" is the contraction for "it is." To test usage, read out loud the sentence you are forming. If you stumble using "it is," then "its" is correct.

Examples:
Ray told his children, "Its time to leave for the park." (no)
Ray told his children, "It's time to leave for the park." (yes)
The school was proud of it's principal. (no)
The school was proud of its principal. (yes)

20. I'm confused about how to indicate the possessive of words ending in "s". Help please.

Typically, if a word ends in "s," and the word is singular, add an apostrophe and an "s" to the end. This may look awkward, but it is correct. If the word is plural and ends in "s", simply add the apostrophe.

Examples:
Jack Nicklaus' wife shouted "hooray" when he sank the winning putt. (no)
Jack Nicklaus's wife shouted "hooray" when he sank the winning putt. (yes)
James Johnsons' girls decided to try out for the play. (no)
James Johnson's girls decided to try out for the play. (yes)

21. When should I use ellipses and how should they be spaced?

Ellipsis points serve a dual purpose: to indicate missing words in a sentence or to permit a sentence to trail off without an ending. Proper usage requires leaving a space after the word before the use of the ellipses and before the next word once

the ellipses have been used. If one is used after a complete sentence, a fourth dot is used to represent the period.

Examples:
This is a fine mess. . . . Get the hell out of here. (no)
President Roosevelt said, "We have nothing to fear . . . but fear itself." (yes)
"Romeo," she called, "let me explain . . . " (yes)

22. Do I leave one space or two after a complete sentence and the beginning of the next one?

It is now correct to use one space after a period when using word processing programs. For those of you who love the typewriter, two spaces are permissible.

23. What is the correct punctuation to be used with parentheses?

Punctuation is positioned after the use of the closing parenthesis. If the material inside the parenthesis requires its own punctuation, position it accordingly.

Examples:
Alex ran toward Felix, (a half-breed) who scampered away. (no)
Alex ran toward Felix (a half-breed), who scampered away. (yes)
The best of times (why should it be questioned?), bring out the best in man. (yes)

24. Should I indent each paragraph, and if so, how many spaces? Also – should there be spaces between my paragraphs?

Publishers' requirements vary, but the current trend is to add a line space between paragraphs and use no indentation.

Examples:
See writing samples in Appendix.

25. What in the world are split infinitives? Do I need them?

Stay away from them or you will be shot. Infinitives are verbs that have a "to" in front of them like "to catch," or "to think." The trouble arises when words such as "so," "really," and other "ly" words separate the "to" from the verb. This causes a split infinitive and is unacceptable.

Examples:
Jimmy loves apples, but loves to also eat bananas (no).
Jimmy loves apples, but he also loves to eat bananas (yes).
Ben and Jerry wanted to really watch the television program. (no).
Ben and Jerry really wanted to watch the television program. (yes)

26. I think exclamation points are nifty. Is it okay to use them?

Less rather than more is the standard rule. Too many exclamation points provide a hint that you are not a professional writer. Never use !!!!!! – it is totally unprofessional. One exclamation point is all you need, if that, since your writing should show enough emotion through strong word choice.

Examples:
I love to ice skate!!!!!! (no)
Freddie won first prize! (yes)
Black Sox slept with a grin on his face! (yes)
Sally exclaimed, "What an exciting game!" (yes)

Miscellaneous Tips

Never use "%" in text, but rather spell out "percent." It is alright to use the symbol in illustrations or charts.

Never us "&" in text unless it is part of a logo or business name. Always spell out the word "and."

Avoid using overused or trite phrases such as “the fact that,” “is a person who,” “as to whether,” or “in regard to.” They sound like filler and add only unnecessary verbiage.

Be careful not to use “of” where “have” is required. “Phil should have gone to the market,” is proper while “Phil should of gone to the market” is not.

Helpful Reminders:

Good writing requires hard work even for the best wordsmiths. Many best-selling authors and poets have spent years writing one book.

There are few absolutes regarding grammar and punctuation rules in the publishing industry, but rather accepted standards and conventions. This book has presented universally accepted guidelines, but be certain to check the style guide used by the publishing company you are submitting your material to.

Remember – typos and other errors tend to cluster. If you find one mistake, read each sentence around it and you’ll likely discover more.

Reading your text out loud is a good way to discover errors. Another is to wait a few days after you have composed material and then look at it with a fresh perspective.

Better yet, have a professional proofreader scan the text before any submission. This will enhance your chances for a mistake-free manuscript.

Poetry Punctuation and Grammar

Poetry Consciousness: Punctuation and the Linebreak

The Importance of Punctuation

Punctuation is defined as the use of standardized marks and signs in writing to separate words into sentences, clauses, and phrases in order to clarify meaning. This seems simple when you are dealing with paragraphs. But poetry is another matter altogether. It begs the question, is there a *right way* to use punctuation in poetry?

The answer is no, but while there is not a right way, there is a best way.

Punctuation is used to summarize thoughts and ideas, to aid in lucidity and the manifestation of meaning, and especially to signal when and where to pause. Poetry may very well be a different animal from prose, but punctuation, because of its formulaic nature, serves the same function in both forms.

With this in mind, it is easier to understand why punctuation is so important. The same can be said about the linebreak. Poets have the power to break lines to emphasize several different logics. A line may be broken to emphasize an end word; the poet may chose to break a line in order to enjamb (changing the meaning of both the line after and preceding the break); a line may be broken to adhere to a rhythm or rhyme scheme.

To the poet, the craft of creating a poem is a process of precision. Every word, every linebreak, every punctuation mark is an essential element in helping the reader come to a conclusion about the meaning of the poem. By not taking punctuation seriously, by not knowing some of the basic rules of punctuation or by randomly choosing places at which to break lines, poets may unwittingly lead the reader astray and leave a plethora of room for an incorrect interpretation of the sentiment.

Robert Frost once said, "Poetry is a way to take life by the throat." This idea, that poetry is a powerful medium for grasping the essentials of living, is a clear sign that poetry is not an art form to be taken lightly. We must be conscious of every move, we must be diligent, awake, and aware of the logics we implore in every line of every poem we write.

Poetic Forms

Most poetic forms require punctuation. It is difficult to understand how punctuation is used without a sense of how to look at a poem. Become familiar with different forms of poetry, their rhyme schemes (if there is one). The process of analyzing verse into metrical patterns is called scanning. Here is a list of several formal types of poems. Use the definitions to gain a better understanding of logics by which lines are broken and how punctuation may be used.

The **sonnet** is a poetic form characterized by fourteen lines of iambic penameter and a rhyme scheme. This form has several variations including the Italian, Petrachan, and others.

Tanka is a Japanese form of poetry with five lines. Line one has five syllables, line two has seven, line three has five, and lines four and five have seven syllables each, making a total of 31 syllables.

A **limerick** is a light verse form of poetry containing five lines. The first, second, and last lines scan like this: weak STRONG weak weak STRONG weak weak STRONG, and the third and fourth scan like this: weak STRONG weak weak STRONG'.

The **triolet** is a French form of poetry with eight lines. The first, fourth, and seventh lines are identical. So are the second and eighth lines. It usually is written in a combination of iambic tetrameter and trimeter.

The **villanelle** is 19 lines and six stanzas long. There are two rhyming sounds with a rhyme scheme like this: aba aba aba aba aba abaa. Here's the confusing part: the first and third lines of the first stanza are repeated in alternation—the first line is the last line of the second stanza, the third line is the last line of the third stanza, etc. And the first and third lines are the third and fourth lines, respectively, in the last stanza.

The **pantoum** is a form of Asian poetry and is unique in its repetition. The second and fourth lines of every stanza are the first and third of the next, and the second and fourth lines of the final stanza happen to be the first and third lines of the first stanza, giving a 'circle' effect.

The **sestina** has seven stanzas, six with six lines and one with three lines. The six words that end the first stanza's lines are repeated at the end of the lines in the first six stanzas. The final stanza uses two of these "key words" per line.

The **ballade** is a form of poetry containing three eight-line stanzas and an envoy which may be either four or five lines long. The last line of the first stanza is the last line of all others, including the envoy. There are only three rhyming sounds, and no word can be repeated as a rhyme.

The **paradelle** resembles a word puzzle. There are six lines per stanza. In all stanzas but the last, the first four lines are two different lines repeated twice, and the last two lines use all the words of the previous line. The last stanza uses all the words of the previous stanzas.

This **rondeau** is French in origin and contains 13 lines. It is built on two rhymes. What is unique about this form is that the first few words of the first line are repeated as the last lines of the next stanzas.

Since the establishment of **free verse**, a form most closely aligned with such American and English poets as Ezra Pound, Amy Lowell, T.S. Eliot, and Walt Whitman, an enormous variety of rhythms and forms have been explored. Each poem has the possibility of its own irregular music, its own unusual shape and form, and a great deal of experimentation with linebreak and punctuation.

Standard Punctuation Marks

For your review, here are a few standard punctuation marks, their usages and an example or two of how each of these points is applied in poetry:

The **comma**— A punctuation mark (,) used to indicate a separation of ideas or of elements within the structure of a sentence.

- A pause or separation; a caesura.
- Use a comma before the words "and" and "or" in a series of three or more, e.g., Walt Whitman's poem "Song of Myself."

  It may be you are from old people, or from offspring taken,
  It may be if I had known them I would have loved them,
  soon out of their mother's laps,
  And here you are the mothers' laps.

- Follow a statement that introduces a direct quotation of one or more paragraphs with a comma. But use a colon after "as follows."
  Examples: Dorothy Parker's epitaph reads, "Pardon my dust."
  Dorothy Parker's epitaph reads as follows: "Pardon my dust."

- Introductory words such as "to wit," "namely," "i.e.," "e.g.," and "viz" should be immediately preceded and followed by a comma.
  Examples: International students are required to submit proof of identity,

- e.g., a passport, immunization record, a visa, or some other form of identification.

The **semicolon**— A mark of punctuation (;) used to connect independent clauses and indicating a closer relationship between the clauses than a comma or period does.

- Look at the use of the semicolon in the first stanza of Elizabeth Bishop's poem "One Art"

  The art of losing isn't hard to master;
  so many things seem filled with the intent
  to be lost that their loss is no disaster.

The **colon**— A punctuation mark (:) used after a word introducing a quotation, an explanation, an example, or a series and often after the salutation of a business letter.

- Consider this section from Margaret Atwood's poem, "**Spelling.**" Notice the use of the colon in the second stanza show here:

  I return to the story
  of the woman caught in the war
  & in labour, her thighs tied
  together by the enemy
  so she could not give birth.

  Ancestress: the burning witch,
  her mouth covered by leather
  to strangle words.

The **dash**— A line, approximately the width of two hyphens (—) used in writing or printing, denoting a sudden break, stop, or transition in a sentence, or an abrupt change in its construction, a long or significant pause, or an unexpected or epigrammatic turn of sentiment. Dashes are also sometimes used instead of commas or parentheses.

- In Emily Dickinson's poem "Ah , Moon— and Star!" notice her use of the dash in the first stanza of the poem:

Ah, Moon—and Star!
You are very far—
But were no one
Farther than you—
Do you think I'd stop
For a Firmament—
Or a Cubit—or so?

The **hyphen**—A punctuation mark (-) used between the parts of a compound word or name or between the syllables of a word, especially when divided at the end of a line of text

Parenthesis—Either or both of the upright curved lines, ( ), used to mark off explanatory or qualifying remarks in writing or printing.

A qualifying or amplifying word, phrase, or sentence inserted within written matter in such a way as to be independent of the surrounding grammatical structure.

A comment departing from the theme of discourse; a digression.

- Look at the interesting and ingenious use of the parentheses in this poem:

1(a...(a leaf falls on loneliness)
e.e. cummings

1(a

le
af
fa
ll

s)
one
l

ness

The **apostrophe**— The superscript sign (') used to indicate abbreviations to show where a letter or letters are omitted , the possessive case, or the plurals of letters.

The **quotation mark**— Either of a pair of punctuation marks used primarily to mark the beginning and end of a passage attributed to another and repeated word for word, but also to indicate meanings and to indicate the unusual or dubious status of a word. They appear in the form of double quotation marks (“ ”) and single quotation marks (‘ ’). Single quotation marks are usually reserved for setting off a quotation within another quotation in double quotation marks.

The **exclamation point**— A punctuation mark (!) used after an exclamation. Also called **exclamation mark**.

- Take a look at the last stanza of the poem “Ah, Moon— and Star!” by Emily Dickinson:

  But, Moon, and Star,
  Though you're very far—
  There is one—farther than you—
  He—is more than a firmament—from Me—
  So I can never go!

The **question mark**— A punctuation symbol (?) written at the end of a sentence or phrase to indicate a direct question. Also called **interrogation point**.

The **period**— A punctuation mark (.) indicating a full stop, placed at the end of declarative sentences and other statements thought to be complete, and after many abbreviations.

The Linebreak and Punctuation

Realizing that the main difference between poetry and prose is the linebreak inspires the interesting question of how the linebreak should or should not influence punctuation. Traditionally the linebreak has indicated a break or pause and each line has aspired to produce an effect, a work of art all alone. Therefore each line usually contained one or more types of punctuation serving as ques on where to break, where to breath, and what thought, image, emotion, and/or object to emphasize; a key of sorts for each line. This aspiration has forced poets to make conscious decisions on when, where and why to break a line. But what happens when the line becomes more of a way to punctuate than a way to contain? In the last two hundred years poetry has changed dramatically, therefore the linebreak and poetic punctuation have too evolved.

Conventionally, punctuation has indicated the pace of a poem, but take a look at the third stanza of Walt Whitman's poem "Song of Myself."

My tongue, every atom of my blood, form'd from this soil, this air,
Born here of parents born here from parents the same, and their
parents the same,
I, now thirty-seven years old in perfect health begin,
Hoping to cease not till death.

You will notice that Whitman's long lines indicate a slower, listier pace. The commas give you pause to breath.

In Gwendolyn Brooks poem "We Real Cool" notice how she uses enjambment and anticipatory linebreaking to emphasis lines that appear following the "We" in each line. This increases the energy and momentum of the poem.

We Real Cool
Gwendolyn Brooks

We real cool. We
Left School. We

Lurk late. We
Strike straight. We

Sing sin. We
Thin gin. We

Jazz June. We
Die soon.

Linebreak Logics

Consider Steve Kowits' book, *In the Palm of Your Hand.* He reviews the different logics poets use to break their lines.

Linebreaks, in strong poetry, are not random, they serve the poem, meaning they follow a logical pattern and emphasis or de-emphasis of words or phrasing. Good linebreaks make rhythmic, syllabic and serial sense.

Kowit lists the following "logics" for breaking lines in a poem. These are not rules, rather, but observations.

Some poets use a linebreak to end a phrase or sentence (with accompanying punctuation). This is the most obvious reason to break a line. Notice how William Blake's poem, "The Sick Rose," uses this logic in the first two lines and last line of the poem:

The Sick Rose
William Blake

O Rose thou art sick.
The invisible worm.
That flies in the night
In the howling storm:

Has found out thy bed
Of crimson joy:
And his dark secret love
Does thy life destroy.

Poets often use a linebreak for pace or to break up rhythm. In the first stanza of the Pablo Neruda poem "Poetry," notice that often Neruda's lines do not end when a phrase is complete, but rather to propel the momentum of the poem forward:

And it was at that age...Poetry arrived
in search of me. I don't know, I don't know where
it came from, from winter or a river.
I don't know how or when,
no, they were not voices, they were not
words, nor silence,
but from a street I was summoned,

from the branches of night,
abruptly from the others,
among violent fires
or returning alone,
there I was without a face
and it touched me.

Sometimes poets break a line to stress the last word of the line. This is called end word emphasis. In Lucille Clifton's poem "Good Times," notice that she uses strong words like "rent" and "gone" and "hit" at the end of almost every line:

Good Times
Lucille Clifton

my daddy has paid the rent
and the insurance man is gone
and the lights is back on
and my uncle brud has hit
for one dollar straight
and they is good times
good times
good times

my mama has made bread
and grampaw has come
and everybody is drunk
and dancing in the kitchen
and dancing in the kitchen
of these is good times

good times
good times

oh children think about the
good times

The previous poem is also a good example of another logic used to break lines. Sometimes poets will use a linebreak in lieu of punctuation. Notice that in the second stanza of "Good Times," a linebreak takes the place of the comma in this series of actions. Poets will use the linebreak in short lines to slow pace of the poem.

Emily Dickinson's poem, "Ah, Moon—And Stars" deliberately breaks each line into shorter phrases to encourage readers to slow down.

Ah Moon—And Star!
Emily Dickinson
240

Ah, Moon—and Star!
You are very far—
But were no one
Farther than you—
Do you think I'd stop
For a Firmament—
Or a Cubit—or so?

I could borrow a Bonnet
Of the Lark—
And a Chamois' Silver Boot—
And a stirrup of an Antelope—
And be with you—Tonight!

But, Moon, and Star,
Though you're very far—
There is one—farther than you—
He—is more than a firmament—from Me—
So I can never go!

Poets will use the linebreak to invoke surprise, irony or tension. Consider this interesting poem by e. e. cummings. In this poem, she uses the linebreak to break up letters in order to express loneliness.

1(a... (a leaf falls, loneliness)
e.e. cummings

1(a

le
af

fa
ll

s)
one
l
iness

Poet's use the linebreak in order to enjamb. Enjambment is a poet concept describing the metamorphosis of lines on top of lines. For example, one line may have a different meaning alone than when connected to the line right under it. Consider Margaret Atwood's poem "Spelling." She uses enjambment to alter the meanings of lines by attaching them to surprising uses of the word "spell." Notice in the last two sections of this poem how enjambment is used to change the meaning of lines:

Spelling
Margaret Atwood

My daughter plays on the floor
with plastic letters,
red, blue & hard yellow,
learning how to spell,
spelling,
how to make spells.
*
I wonder how many women
denied themselves daughters,
closed themselves in rooms,
drew the curtains
so they could mainline words.
*
A child is not a poem,
a poem is not a child.
There is no either / or.
However.
*

I return to the story
of the woman caught in the war
& in labour, her thighs tied
together by the enemy
so she could not give birth.

Ancestress: the burning witch,
her mouth covered by leather
to strangle words.

A word after a word
after a word is power.

*

At the point where language falls away
from the hot bones, at the point
where the rock breaks open and darkness
flows out of it like blood, at
the melting point of granite
when the bones know
they are hollow & the word
splits & doubles & speaks
the truth & the body
itself becomes a mouth.

This is a metaphor.

*

How do you learn to spell?
Blood, sky & the sun,
your own name first,
your first naming, your first name,
your first word.

Poet's often use linebreaks to create a picture through the shape of the lines. Refer to the e. e. cummings poem on the previous pages. Notice that cummings uses the letters to "draw" a picture of a leaf falling.

Here are other logics for breaking lines. See if you can find some examples of these in various forms of poetry.

- Breaking lines to maintain parallel grammatical structures of lines.
- Breaking lines to include internal rhyme or external (think formal poetics).

- Breaking lines to preserve linebreak length (syllabic or aesthetic).
- Breaking lines to highlight a series of anaphoric phrases. Consider Gwendolyn Brook's poem "We Real Cool." An anaphoric phrase is a repeated or chant-like phrase. Can you identify the anaphoric word, phrase or parallel grammatical structure in this poem?

  We Real Cool
  Gwendolyn Brooks

  We real cool. We
  Left School. We

  Lurk late. We
  Strike straight. We

  Sing sin. We
  Thin gin. We

  Jazz June. We
  Die soon.

Linebreaking is an art and learning how and when to break a line is as important as what words you use. Being conscious of your linebreaks and of the punctuation you use is an important step in becoming a serious poet.

Punctuation and Linebreak Consciousness

Good poetry is not emotional in its mechanics. This doesn't mean good poetry isn't emotional, but rather conscious control over punctuation and logical choices in linebreaks highlight the emotional content of the poem.

Proper use of punctuation in a poem cannot be overemphasized. Robert Frost's line, "Poetry is a way to take life by the throat," harbors the hope that every word, mark, and linebreak will be essential to the integrity, effectiveness and artistry of the craft. Use punctuation as a tool to show your reader the meaning in your poem. Becoming

conscious of every point, mark and linebreak you use in every line of a poem leads to your becoming a more talented poet.

Writing For Publication

Writing For Publication

In *Elements of Style*, E. B. White explains, "Write with nouns and verbs, not with adjectives and adverbs." Thus begins the word choice process, a defining one for aspiring authors and poets. Used with proper punctuation and grammar, words are the explosive tool of the writer, the means to telling their story in the most powerful way.

In case you never studied the proper use of words included in the English language, or you have forgotten everything you ever learned, here is a primer featuring a few helpful hints regarding word use.

Sentences

A sentence is a complete thought. At the least, it will contain a subject (noun) and a predicate verb phrase that asserts something about or with the noun.

Nouns

Common Nouns – words describing people, places, and things.
(cow, woman, tree)

Proper Nouns – describe a specific person, place, or thing.
(Sid, Governor Newman, Golden Gate Bridge)

Collective Nouns – describe groups of people, places, or things
(congregation, gang, congressmen)

Possessive Nouns – describes possessive case of nouns
(Fred's, minister's, father's, students', gang's)

Pronouns

Used to replace a noun or another pronoun.

There are several types of pronouns (including personal, possessive, demonstrative).

The most common are I, me, mine, my, you, your, yours, she, her, hers, he, him, his, and it. Derivatives include: himself, herself, themselves, itself, someone, other, no one, somebody, something, everything, and everyone.

(Ron understood that he was to speak at the annual meeting.)

(Arlene threw herself at the intruder and knocked him into the wall.)

Verbs

Verbs are used to describe action or a state of being. Four basic types of verbs exist: action verbs, linking verbs, helping verbs, and verb phrases.

Action Verbs – move forward the action taken by the subject

(Jerry drove his damaged white car to the cemetery.)

Linking Verbs – verbs that link the subject and predicate

Common linking verbs – become, be, was, were, is, have been, are, and am.

(He and Sally are leaving for the beach.)

Helping Verbs - Used to make a verb's meaning more clear.

Common helping verbs – should, may, will, has, had, would, and might

(Rusty should have been excused from football practice.)

Conjunctions

Connecting words and providing a relationship between them is the function of conjunctions. Three types exist: coordinating conjunctions, correlative conjunctions, and subordinating conjunctions. Definitions are best related through examples:

Coordinating Conjunctions – and, or, nor, but, for, yet, and so
(Sammy and Rachel went to the movies.)

Correlative Conjunctions – either/or, neither/nor, both/and, not only, but also
(Either let me see your face, or leave immediately.)

Subordinating Conjunctions – Include since, if, though, when, and as long as
(He will be the batboy as long as he behaves himself.)

Prepositions

A preposition links a noun to another word in the sentence. Common prepositions include: beside, across, as, inside, near, off, over, of, except, like, along, at, beyond, and onto.
(He found the right gift for his wife under a pile of merchandise.)

Adjectives

Descriptive words that add flavor to writing. They should be used sparingly. If an adjective is required to describe a noun, then perhaps a better noun can be used.
(The golden ring glowed in the sun.)
(Oregon potatoes are better than Idaho potatoes.)

Adverbs

Descriptive words that describe verbs and adverbs. To be used even more sparingly than adjectives. If an adverb is required, there is more than likely a better verb that can be used. Most adverbs can be spotted by their telltale "ly" ending.

(The manager was emphatically waving at the umpire to gain his attention.)

Aspiring authors and poets unfamiliar with usage of the above tools should consider further education in this area since proper usage forms the building blocks for any type of writing. A good understanding of the mechanics underscores the ability to tell the story in a meaningful way to ensure incorrect language will not be prohibitive to meaning.

Once these skills are mastered, consider the tense to be utilized in telling your story. Many writers confuse readers when they bounce back and forth between tenses. This is to be differentiated from "person" (first, second, or third person) discussed in a previous section. Tense choice needs to be consistent. If you are telling the story in the present tense, (what is happening now), then stay there and don't mix this tense with past tense, a recollection of what was happening in the past. Text included in the Overview (non-fiction), or Synopsis (fiction) section of Book Proposals as described in *Book Report* should be in present tense. This provides a sense of immediacy as the author or poet "shows," not "tells," readers what the novel or work of non-fiction is about.

A good understanding of the terms above regarding word description and a similar understanding of tense choice leads to the challenge of focusing on what specific words are going to be used. With that in mind, here are several tips regarding this selection process excerpted from *Book Report, Publishing Strategies, Writing Tips, and 101 Literary Ideas For Aspiring Authors and Poets*.

The Writing Process

There is nothing more personal than writing. Thoughts originating in the deep recesses of the mind are unique. When these ideas are reduced to writing, they become a direct reflection of one's spiritual and intellectual being.

Those who choose to write professionally must do so with passion and a sense of responsibility since their words will affect the reader's mindset. Thoughts and ideas expressed verbally flutter through the air like multi-colored butterflies and seldom are accurately recalled. A famous psychologist once stated that people don't comprehend the substance of spoken words unless they are repeated six or seven times. Written words expressing thoughts and ideas are more likely to be recalled since readers choose quiet time to enjoy the very essence of published works. **Authors and poets have the opportunity, in a day and age when people don't listen, to inspire, inform, challenge, and entertain whether they write fiction, non-fiction, or a collection of poetry.**

For those choosing to pursue a writing career at an early age, the battle plan is clear: keep an open mind and absorb everything life has to offer. For suggestions on how to be more creative, read *Pencil Dancing, New Ways to Free Your Creative Spirit* by Mari Messer.

Formal education is available through writing classes, books on writing, seminars, and college courses. Search for competent instructors with traditional publishing credits or outstanding academic skills.

To bolster the ability to write with sufficient knowledge, the aspiring writer must garner a sense of history, of what occurred to alter the course of mankind and why. Studying psychology, philosophy, history, and classical literature provides a solid foundation.

Extensive travel is the comrade of good writers. Spanning the globe opens the door to a rich heritage. Sojourns to Greece, Egypt, Italy, England, France, and many other countries are valuable. Asked his advice for young writers, William Faulkner stated, "Travel and read."

While visiting foreign countries, learn about the people, the history, and the customs. Working in a foreign country provides a wealth of knowledge. Don't shy away from what might be considered taboo employment. Faulkner wrote, "The best job ever offered to me was to become a landlord in a brothel."

Writing workshops, seminars, and writers' conferences are meat and potatoes if writing professionally is your goal. They offer the perfect environment in which to gather valuable tips and nuances from those who have achieved the goal of being published. Many such events are publicized in independent, creative-arts-oriented newspapers such as *The Village Voice*.

If you decide later in life that writing is a profession of choice, the alternatives differ. Workshops, seminars, and conferences are valuable tools for learning, but a crash course on writing professionally is a prerequisite if you have not exercised this skill in many years.

Having no formal training, I relied on others to assist me when I began to write *Down For The Count*, the book investigating the Mike Tyson trial. Colleagues with backgrounds in literature and English perused the manuscript as well. I did the best I could with what I knew at the time.

Education is essential to learning the craft of writing, but those who proclaim that someone with no formal literary training cannot succeed should recall the background of no less a "scholar" than William Shakespeare. While he was schooled in Greek and Latin literature, rhetoric, and Christian ethics, there is no evidence that the Bard was ever taught the art of writing. History indicates he left school at age fifteen, never pursued further formal education, and was not considered a learned man. This did not prohibit him from writing what many experts consider to be the most extraordinary body of works in the history of literature.

Poet Walt Whitman further proves that formal training is not linked to literary success. His formal education ended at age eleven. Unlike other writers of his time who enjoyed structured, classical educations at private schools, Whitman learned about writing in the local library. He then joined a newspaper, *The New York Mirror,* where he wrote his first article in 1834. Less than two decades later, after dabbling in short-story fiction, Whitman wrote the classic, *Leaves of Grass.*

Regardless of the success enjoyed by authors such as Shakespeare and Whitman, my path toward becoming an author would have been less cumbersome had I spent more time learning the craft. At the time, my sole intent was to have book after book published to earn a living and avoid traveling far from home. This was a goal since I had become the stepfather of four young children, including triplet boys, at the ripe age of forty-four. Writing professionally was the link to spending quality time with the kids as they grew up.

If you are the "I just decided to take up writing and I want to be published" type as I was, then become an avid reader and practice writing. In his book *On Writing*, famed author Stephen King stated, **"If you want to be a writer, you must do two things above all others—read a lot and write a lot."** Best-selling romance writer Nora Roberts echoes King's sentiments. She began her career as a stay-at-home mother who wrote ideas in a notebook during a snowstorm in 1979. Pleased with her efforts, she continued to write. The result was her first published work, *Irish Thoroughbred.* Since then she has written several bestsellers, all because, as she says, "I don't believe in waiting for inspiration. It's my job to sit down . . . and write."

Whether you are interested in writing fiction or non-fiction, you should read both. Read the classics—Hemingway, Joyce, Dickens, and Steinbeck. Poets can learn from Whitman, Frost, Edgar Allen Poe, and Edna St. Vincent Millay. Each of these great writers admits their education about writing was influenced by the books they read. Asked what authors he enjoyed, Hemingway listed more than thirty-four before confessing that to list them all "would take a day to remember." Among them were Mark Twain, Bach, Tolstoy, Dostoevsky, Chekhov, Kipling,

Shakespeare, and Dante. Hemingway admitted he also gained education from artists and composers. "I learned as much from painters about how to write," he stated, "as from writers . . . I should think that what one learns from composers and from the study of harmony and counterpoint would be obvious."

Competent authors are superb storytellers. While reading the classics, note how the canonized authors weave a story. Whether the choice is fiction or non-fiction, the story must be clear, have a good beginning, middle, and end, and never be boring. Reading well-written books helps you realize how others have accomplished the feat. In *On Writing*, Stephen King states:

> Good writing . . . teaches the learning writer about style, graceful narration, plot development, the creation of believable characters, and truth-telling. A novel like *Grapes of Wrath* may fill a new writer with feelings of despair and good, old-fashioned jealousy—I'll never be able to write anything that good, not if I live to be a thousand—but such feelings can also serve as a spur, goading the writer to work harder and aim higher. **Being swept away by a combination of great story and great writing . . . is a part of every writer's necessary formation.** You cannot hope to sweep someone else away by the force of your writing until it has been done to you.

In *Bird by Bird*, by Anne Lamott, the author presents an interesting strategy regarding fiction storytelling. Lamott quotes Alice Adams from a lecture about short story writing. The excerpt reads:

> [Alice] said that sometimes she uses a formula when writing a short story, which goes ABDCE, for Action, Background, Development, Climax, and Ending. You begin with action that is compelling enough to draw us in, make us want to know more. Background is where you let us see and know who these people are, how they've come to be together, what was going on before the opening of the story. Then you develop these people, so that we learn what they care most care about. The plot – the drama, the actions, the tension – will grow out of that. You move them along until everything comes together in the climax, after which things are different for the main characters, different in some real way. And then there is the ending: what is our sense of who these people are now, what they are left with, what happened, and what did it mean.

Fiction writers can learn from Scott Turow, author of several bestsellers, including *Presumed Innocent*. An excerpt reads:

The atomized life of the restaurant spins on about us. At separate tables, couples talk; the late-shift workers dine alone; the waitresses pour coffee. And here sits Rusty Sabich, thirty-nine years old, full of lifelong burdens and workaday fatigue. I tell my son to drink his milk. I nibble at my burger. Three feet away is the woman whom I have said I've loved for nearly twenty years, making her best efforts to ignore me.

Besides being a terrific storyteller, character description was Jack Kerouac's specialty. An excerpt of *On The Road* reads:

He was a gray, nondescript-looking fellow you wouldn't notice on the street, unless you looked closer and saw his mad, bony skull with its strange youthfulness – a Kansas minister with exotic, phenomenal fires and mysteries. He had studied medicine in Vienna; had studied anthropology, read everything; and now he was settling to his life's work, which was the study of things themselves in the streets of life and the night.

In *Balzac and the Little Chinese Seamstress*, author Dai Sijie sweeps the reader into his novel portraying life during China's Cultural Revolution. An except reads:

The room served as shop, workplace, and dining room all at once. The floorboards were grimy and streaked with yellow-and-black gobs of dried spittle left by clients. You could tell they were not washed down daily. There were hangers with finished garments suspended on a string across the middle of the room. The corners were piled high with bolts of material and folded clothes, which were under siege from an army of ants.

Providing a good beginning, middle, and end to a story by doing so with each paragraph provides excellent storytelling. In *Down and Out In London and Paris*, George Orwell presents a worthy example. The excerpt reads:

The Jew delivered the cocaine the same day, and promptly vanished. And meanwhile, as was not surprising after the fuss Roucolle had made, the affair had been noised all over the quarter. The very next morning the hotel was raided and searched by the police.

In the non-fiction bestseller, *Seabiscuit*, author Laura Hillenbrand captures the reader's attention by providing visual and dramatic scenes propelling the reader into the middle of the action. An excerpt reads:

> A minute later the field bent around the far turn and rushed at the grandstand. There was one horse in front and pouring it on. His silks were red. It was Seabiscuit. The crowd roared. Pollard [the jockey] and Seabiscuit glided down the lane all by themselves, reaching the wire in track-record-equaling time. Kayak was right behind them. It was Pollard's first win since 1938.

Journals and Idea Books

Learning the craft of writing is a continuing process. One of the best means to hone the craft is by writing in a journal or diary. It promotes discipline while providing a chronology of your life.

Author John Fowles (*The French Lieutenant's Woman*) stated, "I am a great believer in diaries, if only in the sense that bar exercises are good for ballet dancers; it's often through personal diaries that the novelist discovers his true bent." This comment is applicable for non-fiction writers as well.

One exercise to consider requires writing in a journal each day for a week. Content and length are optional, but the goal is to complete the task. Then cast aside the journal for a few days before reading it. If you're satisfied with the text, and the process involved, then you have the potential to write professionally. If you hate what you wrote, and the discipline of having to write each day, then consider basketry, modern art, or some other means of expending creative energy.

Another useful exercise is to organize a folder containing observations about others. Good writers are people watchers. Whether you do so in a park, at sports events, or at a bus stop, chronicle your thoughts and observations. Vivid description and words evoking emotion are the earmarks of the good writer. To enhance this skill, study speech patterns, how people move, what habits they possess, and face and body features. Make lists of these characteristics; then add other elements. A fat notebook I often refer to includes pages listing names (Avon Privette, Paris Wolfe, Tootie Witmer, Audrey Wink, Holly Furfer, Bobby April, David Duck), smells (bug spray, moth balls, fresh strawberry pie, chemical fertilizer), descriptions (salty, speckled, overripe, furry), hair style (butch, raggedy, ponytail, mousy), and body parts (webbed feet, spindly toes, stubby arms, firm butt, limp face, spidery fingers, slumping posture, drooping eyes, artificial eyes, whiskey nose, parched lips, dead legs). Another list includes weather descriptions (gray drizzle, sideways rain, Oklahoma wind) and sky descriptions (primrose, veined with dry lightning, streaky blue).

In a nother section of my "help" book, one added to on a daily basis, I list "useful phrases." Included is soft laughter, hushed giggle, black scuff marks, pocket change, replied indifferently, fork patrol, pigeon toed, steady gaze, shimmered in the moonlight, and crumpled pompadour.

Before beginning the writing process, consult your lists and permit words and ideas to fill your brain with creativity. Clever words and phrases spice up the text, providing the reader with the all-important asset that E. B. White emphasizes: **visualization**. Learned author John Cheever endorsed White's viewpoint when he stated, "The books you really love give the sense, when you first open them, of having been there. It is a creation, almost like a chamber in the memory. Places that one has never been to, things that one has never seen or heard, but their fitness is so sound that you've been there somehow."

Having gained the essential skills necessary to write well, the aspiring author or poet is in pursuit of a realistic goal: being published. A good book idea plus an excellent strategy plus hard work permits this goal to be realized.

Word Usage

While reading, note the author or poet's word choice. There are those who love the vocabulary and appreciate hundred-dollar words that claim, "I'm a literate son-of-a-gun with a graduate degree in Webster's." But language must never be vague, elusive, or downright inaccessible. A story loses much of its flow and meaning if the reader spends too much time opening a dictionary. Phrases like "revelatory episodes," "epigrammatic prose," and "diorama of American plenty" will confuse and dismay 95 percent of the population.

Throughout my tenure as an author, readers have provided feedback indicating that my books are "easily read." Little highbrow language exists in my books because I purposely exclude words preventing the flow of the language. I want to make them stop and think or enjoy the text, not be impressed with my use of big words.

Doing so is essential if you want to reach a broad readership, because **writing is personal, not only for the *writer*, but for the *reader*.** As the writer, you are conveying information regarding a story intended to captivate the reader. You

want your words to leap off the page and infiltrate the reader's brain to entice, excite, entertain, or make them stop and think. When readers purchase a book, it will be successful if they ask, "Who is this author or poet and what is he or she trying to show [not tell] me?"

The *Chicago Manual of Style* is a dense book, and not vacation reading. Set aside ample time so you can focus on its contents. A better idea is to consult the book in spurts, and take notes. Then refer to it again and again like a close friend who tells the truth.

Publishers prefer that authors and poets adhere to the rules presented in this publication, but *Elements of Style*, by William Strunk Jr. and E. B. White, is ninety-five pages long, the perfect length for obtaining good, solid information about writing. Spending less than ten dollars for the book is one of the best investments an aspiring author or poet can make.

Professor Strunk published the classic for his students in 1919. It soon became known as the "little book that could." Over the years, White, most famous for writing *Charlotte's Web,* has revised it for modernization purposes, but the gem features Strunk's brilliant mind probing the depths of writing and what is proper and correct. Under titles such as "Elementary Rules of Usage," "Elementary Rules of Composition," "A Few Matters of Form," and "Words and Expressions Commonly Misused," the Cornell professor provides simple, clear, and brilliant guidelines. Among the jewels are warnings against overuse of adverbs and adjectives, advocacy of active voice and positive words, and rules for positioning pronouns. *Elements of Style* explains the whys and wherefores so even a dunderhead can understand. I recommend putting the book under your pillow while you sleep with the hope that the knowledge will seep into your brain.

While the first four sections of the book are a must-read, E. B. White added Book V, titled "An Approach to Style." He writes, "Up to this point, the book has been concerned with what is correct, or acceptable, in the use of English. In this final chapter, we approach style in its broader meaning: style in the sense of what is distinguished and distinguishing. Here we leave solid ground. Who can confidently say what ignites a certain combination of words, causing them to explode in the mind?"

Regardless of the caveat, White's suggestions *are* on solid ground. Sections include: "Placing yourself in the background," "Write in a way that comes naturally," "Work from a suitable design," and "Write with nouns and verbs, not with adverbs and adjectives." White discusses the need to revise and rewrite, not to overwrite, and not to overstate.

After discovering Strunk and White's book and consulting the *Chicago Manual of Style*, I was pleased to note that much of what they suggested had somehow been incorporated into my writing style. This stemmed from reading what other *good writers* had written . . . and perhaps some *bad writers'* work as well since I learned to discern the gibberish many believed necessary to tell their stories.

Absorbing the lessons outlined in the "little book" provides a basis for developing writing skills. Each author or poet chooses a storytelling method, but proper usage of language guarantees that errors won't signal lack of talent. Editors at publishing companies dismiss a manuscript or collection of poetry if there are misspellings and grammatical errors, but they also pay close attention to word usage.

Learning good writing skills at an early age will benefit aspiring authors and poets. Parents interested in supplemental materials to improve children's writing skills may consider the Shurley English method. More information is available at www.shurley.com.

Clarity

In *On Writing Well*, author William Zinsser states, "Good writing has an aliveness that keeps the reader reading from one paragraph to the next, and it's not a question of gimmicks to 'personalize' the author. It's a question of using the English language in a way that will achieve the greatest clarity and strength."

Fiction writers must ask themselves several questions regarding clarity. Is the story time-oriented so the reader understands the time frame being presented? Are the characters well defined and do they act in a manner consistent with the background provided? Is there a believable backdrop for the story—one that is vivid? Have I written a clever, dramatic story with a ticking clock to add suspense?

Non-fiction writers face a comparable question—will a story that is quite clear to the writer be as clear to the reader? Will the reader understand the message being conveyed by the text? This applies to poets as well.

Author John Updike provided a guidepost regarding clarity. He wrote,

"When I write, I aim in my mind not toward New York, but toward a vague spot a little to the east of Kansas. I think of the books on library shelves, without their jackets, years old, and a countryish teenaged boy finding them speak to him." Author Zinsser suggests, "Clutter is the disease of American writing. We are a society strangling in unnecessary words, circular constructions, pompous frills, and meaningless jargon."

As the writing process continues, writers must be certain they have told the story they intend to tell, and with accuracy. Many times we read what our brain *wants* to read instead of what *is* on the page. In a final draft of this book, I credited Robert Frost with writing *Leaves of Grass*. I knew better, but had Frost on the brain. When an editor pointed out the mistake, I was embarrassed.

One method of determining clarity while proofreading for errors is to read the material aloud. By inspecting and hearing each word, meaning becomes clearer and mistakes are revealed that would otherwise have been overlooked.

Writing Skills

Information about how to write and writing style are referenced in many books including *Elements of Style* by professors Strunk and White. White was correct when he wrote that no one understands why a certain group of words carefully joined produce magic on the sheet of paper for one author while resulting in gobbledygook for another. Each writer's composition of words will differ according to his or her skill and experience.

In his book, *On Writing*, Stephen King offers a simple explanation for what he believes is important when considering writing style. He wrote, "Book buyers want a good story to take with them on the airplane, something that will first fascinate them, then pull them in and keep them turning the pages." Mystery writer Tony Hillerman (*Hunting Badger*) told *Writer's Digest*, "I feel my first priority as a writer is to entertain the audience."

Never forget; every book is an adventure. Write it like one. This is true whether you are creating a tortoise and hare story, a book about the inner workings of the latest computer, a chronicle of the evolution of Red Lobster stores as an American success story, a biography of the gifted poet Etheridge Knight, or a collection of poetry about why birds fly south for the winter.

Author James Patterson espouses a unique perspective of writing. In *The Writer's Handbook*, he states, "In the beginning, I really worried a lot about sentences in my books. But at some point . . . I stopped writing sentences and started writing stories. And that's the advice I give to new writers. Sentences are really hard to write. Stories flow. If you've got an idea, the story will flow. Once you have the story down you can go back and polish it for the next ten years."

No one doubts that clear, concise storytelling featuring language that *shows,* but does not *tell,* is paramount to success. Some writers sprinkle flowery language throughout their manuscripts. Others write like Hemingway and produce some sentences that are never-ending. Regardless, the finest writers, whether they are writing fiction, non-fiction, or poetry, are brief and visual, two great talents gained through experience. Being visual means to flavor your writing with the five senses—sight, smell, touch, taste, and hearing—so the reader consumes and is consumed with the text.

Professor Strunk wrote in *The Elements of Style*, "If those who have studied the art of writing are in accord on any one point, it is this: the surest way to arouse and hold the reader's attention is by being specific, definite, and concrete. The greatest writers—Homer, Dante, Shakespeare—are effective because they deal in particulars and report the details that matter. Their words call up pictures." Strunk added, "Vigorous writing is concise. A sentence should contain no unnecessary words, a paragraph no unnecessary sentences, for the same reason that a drawing should have no unnecessary lines and a machine no unnecessary parts."

Author Nora Roberts believes visualization means proper selection and description of characters whether the book is fiction or non-fiction. She told *Writer's Digest,* "Your characters have to jump off the page. They have to appeal to the reader in some way . . . They need to be appealing, humorous and human."

Literary agent Julia Castiglia echoes Roberts' words in *Writer's Digest.* "What we really look for are books that are well written, with a certain zing to them that climbs off the page and wraps itself around our brains, that so entrance and seduce us that we just can't say no."

Word Choice

The requirement that the writer *show* the reader and not *tell* cannot be over-emphasized. Word choice is key. Mark Twain wrote, "The difference between the right word and the nearly right word is the same as that between lightning and lightning bug."

To improve a story, use active words portraying concrete images instead of abstractions: avoid crutch-words ending in "ly"; avoid "not" and "no"; use active verbs like "clawed," "swatted," and "pawed," instead of linking verbs like "is" and "was"; avoid overuse of gerunds (verbs used as nouns by adding "ing"); and use stronger nouns instead of adjectives. Regarding the need for active verbs, author William Zinsser wrote, "Verbs are the most important of all your tools. They push the sentence forward and give it momentum. Active verbs push hard; passive verbs tug fitfully."

Avoid words such as "a little," "very," "kind of," "pretty much" or "really" to qualify other words. They are often unnecessary and make your writing sound trite.

Pay attention to your use of the relative pronouns "that" and "which." They are commonly confused and their misuse is a danger signal to the professional editor since they are not interchangeable. Use "that" to introduce a clause defining a particular noun ("She is terrified of dogs that bark at night"). Use "which" to introduce a clause that simply provides additional detail ("She is terrified of the neighbor's dog, which barks at night."). Notice that "which" is usually preceded by a comma while "that" is not.

Concise word usage translates to appropriate paragraph length. Reader attention span is short, so use of a few sentences separates the text and keeps the flow of the story at a steady pace. Long paragraphs are bulky and can bog down the reader. Avoid them.

Strong word usage is essential at the beginning of a chapter, or a verse. Words completing a chapter or a verse must tantalize and urge the reader onward.

Adverbs and Adjectives

Stephen King's book, *On Writing,* provides several important tips. One suggests a writing mantra to be repeated again and again.

King said, "The adverb is not your friend." He believes if the verb chosen cannot stand on its own, replace it with one that does.

Word choice signals the distinctive voice writers convey in conversation with the reader. How they manipulate certain words into the story dictates the tone of that voice. William Zinsser states, "Bear in mind, when you're choosing words and stringing them together, how they sound. This may seem absurd: readers read with their eyes. But in fact they hear what they are reading far more than you realize. Therefore such matters as rhythm and alliteration are vital to every sentence." Zinsser adds, "Develop one voice that readers will recognize when they hear it on the page, a voice that's enjoyable not only in its musical line but its avoidance of sounds that would cheapen its tone: breeziness and condescension and clichés."

Never one to discount the advice of an author like Stephen King who has sold more books than there are people in China, an "adverb hunt" was commenced during the final edit of my book *Miscarriage of Justice*. To this end, we scoured the manuscript and eliminated 95 percent of the adverbs.

The "word surgery" performed regarding use of adverbs in the book was successful, and the patient lived. Some adverbs can be helpful, but removing the malignant language improved the book considerably.

While editing, we also concentrated on "word brevity," eliminating words not advancing the story. Any time we saw "they were," "they are," "there is," "it is," or "it was," we crossed them out along with dreaded clichés.

Many authors develop an affinity for one word. Mine is "that." I love the word, but often it is not required. During editing of this book, I attempted to eliminate as many "thats" as possible. I'm sure I could delete others, but at least I have spared readers many of my unnecessary, pet words. Be careful though: non-use of a word where it is required can be as bad as overusing it.

Brevity is essential. Without exception, less is better. When Ernest Hemingway was chided for the short length of his classic *Old Man and the Sea*, he answered critics by saying, "[It] could have been over a thousand pages long and had every character in the village in it . . . That is done excellently and well by other writers . . . So I have tried to do something else. First I have tried to eliminate everything unnecessary to convey experience to the reader so that after he or she has read something it will become part of his or her experience and seem actually to have happened. This is very hard to do and I worked at it very hard."

Author Zinsser echoes Hemingway's thoughts. He states,

> **[The] secret of good writing is to strip every sentence to its cleanest components. Every word that serves no function, every long word that could be a short word, every adverb that carries the same meaning that's already in the verb, every passive construction that leaves the reader confused as to who is doing what—these are the thousand and one adulterants that weaken the strength of a sentence.**

Historians recall that brevity was a key to Abraham Lincoln's speeches. During his Second Inaugural Address, he utilized just 701 words. Five hundred five of them were of one syllable; 122 contained two.

To realize that short books are jewels of the writing profession, recall such classics as *The Great Gatsby, The Red Badge of Courage, Turn of the Screw,* and *A Lost Lady. Tuesdays With Morrie* is another. A helpful book for those who love to use run-on sentences is *The Dictionary of Concise Writing: 10,000 Alternatives to Wordy Phrases* by Robert Harwell Fiske.

Run-on sentences permit readers little time to breathe. Early in my career, every paragraph seemed to feature the dreaded run-on. Only by weeding them out, splitting up thoughts, and focusing on being concise have I become a better writer.

Style of writing is an individual matter. It is important to know the standard rules for writing, but many successful authors have broken the rules. Lori Foster, a noted romance author, wrote in *Writer's Digest*, "What really sells your book is your individual voice, not the rules that you obey." Elaborating, she stated, "Just about everyone has heard the dozens and dozens of rules listed as a criteria for getting published in romance. They include: no hopping from one character to another's head, one point of view per scene, no exotic settings, and no athletes or television personalities. In truth, there are very few definite rules."

Truman Capote's thoughts on rules are right on point. He said, "Writing has laws of perspective, of light and shade, just as painting does, or music. If you are born knowing them, fine. If not, learn them. Then rearrange the rules to suit yourself."

While seasoned authors and poets can escape doom with a mistake or two, aspiring authors and poets don't have the luxury. **They must be perfect the first time. If they aren't, dreams of becoming a published author or poet will sift away like the desert sand.**

Keys To The Writing Process

If you decide to write an entire manuscript or collection of poetry before completing a Query Letter and/or Book Proposal, remember one important rule: Once you start, don't stop. The main reason most people who intend to write a book never do is because they encounter a stumbling block regarding word choice, punctuation, or grammar. Before they know it, the creative juices turn sour.

Author and literary guru Natalie Goldberg speaks to this in her book *Writing Down The Bones*. She believes initial thoughts "capture the oddities of your mind." She writes, "First thoughts have tremendous energy. It is the way the mind flashes on something." Author Goldberg provides a list of exercises in her book to inspire writers toward creative thinking.

Author John Steinbeck (*The Grapes of Wrath*) spoke to the importance of completing what you begin. He stated, "Write freely and as rapidly as possible and throw the whole thing on paper. Never correct or rewrite until the whole thing is down. Rewrite in process is usually found to be an excuse for not going on. It also interferes with flow and rhythm which can only come from a kind of unconscious association with the material."

In a 1947 letter to Jack Kerouac, writer Neal Cassady, upon whom Kerouac based the character Dean Moriarty in *On The Road*, wrote:

> I have always held that when one writes, one should forget all rules, literary styles, and other such pretentions as large words, lordly clauses and other phrases as such . . . Rather, I think one should write, as nearly as possible, as if he were the first person on earth and was humbly and sincerely putting on paper that which he saw and experienced and loved and lost; what his passing thoughts were and his sorrows and desires. . .

Actor Sean Connery, playing the part of fictional author William Forrester in *Finding Forrester*, addressed the subject in an interesting manner. He stated, "You write the first draft with your heart. You re-write with your head."

Instead of worrying about mistakes or lapses in the text, plow ahead. There will be time later to fill in the blanks or correct errors. To aid your efforts regarding manuscript form, a Manuscript Techniques list follows this chapter.

Writing Regimen

There is no definitive answer to how much text a writer should complete each day. Stephen King states in his book *On Writing*, "I like to get ten pages a day, which amounts to 2,000 words. That's 180,000 words over a three-month span, a goodish length for a book."

Esteemed author John Updike (*The Power and the Glory*) writes 1,000 words a day, six days a week. This process has resulted in more than fifty books, two of which have earned Pulitzer Prizes.

Ernest Hemingway, who never began writing unless twenty sharpened pencils were close at hand, described his daily routine by stating:

> I write every morning as soon after first light as possible. There is no one to disturb you and it is cool or cold and you come to your work and warm as you write. You read what you have written and, as you always stop when you know what is going to happen next, you go on from there. You write until you come to a place where you still have your juice and know what will happen next and you stop and try to live through until the next day when you hit it again. You have started at six in the morning, say, and may go on until noon or be through before that. When you stop you are as empty, and at the same time never empty but filling, as when you have made love to someone you love.

Poet Maya Angelou's regimen is classic. "I have a hotel room in every town I've ever lived in," she stated. ". . . I leave my home at six, and try to be at work by 6:30. To write, I lie across the bed, so that [my] elbow is absolutely encrusted at the end . . . I stay until 12:30 or 1:30 in the afternoon, and then I go home and try to breathe."

Tom Wolfe (*A Man In Full, The Right Stuff*) sets page goals. He stated, "I set myself a quota—ten pages a day, triple-spaced, which means about eighteen hundred words. If I can finish that up in three hours, I'm through for the day."

Many writers believe they deserve a magnum of champagne in celebration if they can write four to six pages a day. Others write less, some more. It all depends, but never let anything prohibit progress toward the appointed goal. This means the telephone, loved ones, pets, door-to-door salespeople, radio, television, grammar problems, spelling miscues, mosquitoes, or children. All are the writer's enemies since they obstruct completion of the task. My black Labrador's name is Black Sox, but I could name him "Procrastination," since playing ball with him is a tempting diversion from writing.

Block out these enemies, begin to write, then write and write, and write some more. Be sure to "save" the material paragraph by paragraph while working and then save it on a disk when you have completed the day's task so computer "crashes" won't eliminate your text. Mother Nature is another enemy of the writer and her electrical storms are computer killers.

When words are dashing out of the brain, there is exhilaration beyond comprehension. While the juices are flowing, the fingers can't work fast enough. The rush is better than any chemical "high."

Every writer discovers a time and place to write, but my regimen is quite consistent. Being a morning person, I write from just after 5:00 a.m. until 7:30 or so. A quick break to share Rice Krispies with Black Sox breaks up the writing period.

Some days, I am tempted to read my composed material to Black Sox a la John Steinbeck. He wrote, "I've always tried out my material on my dogs first. You know, with Angel, he sits there and listens and I get the feeling he understands everything. But with Charley, I always felt he was just waiting to get a word in edgewise. Years ago, when my red setter chewed up the manuscript of *Of Mice and Men*, I said at the time that the dog must have been an excellent literary critic."

Once breakfast is completed, I walk outside, take a few deep breaths, and then return to the writing table until eleven o'clock. By then, my brain is empty.

Afternoons are set aside for research and a wretched occupation: editing. Most weeks I write every day except for Saturday when I attempt to break par against a great group of buddies at the local golf course. Even then, I carry five-by-seven note cards in case an inspiring thought or observation leaps into my mind.

A proposed regimen is as follows: The writer decides on Sunday to complete the first fifty pages of a manuscript. He or she writes ten pages on Monday and Tuesday, and ten more each on Wednesday, Thursday, and Friday. This night is reserved for celebration, Saturday for recovering from the Friday night hangover, and Sunday for the Sabbath. Poets can adapt a similar regimen for their work.

By not touching the manuscript, the writer will have a fresh perspective on Monday. Best-selling author Truman Capote (*In Cold Blood*) was a proponent of this method. After describing himself as a "horizontal author [who] can't think unless I'm lying down," he stated, "when the yellow draft is finished, I put the manuscript away for a while, a week, a month, sometimes longer. When I take it out again, I read it as coldly as possible, then read it to a friend or two, and decide what changes I want to make."

Revisions

When people ask what I do, I tell them I am a "re-writer," not a writer. This emphasizes how much time is spent revising text.

The process of rewriting is complex. Pulitzer Prize winning author Elie Wiesel stated, "Writing is not like painting, where you add. It is not what you put on the canvas that the reader sees. Writing is more like a sculpture where you remove; you eliminate in order to make the work visible. There is a difference between a book of two hundred pages from the very beginning, and a book of two hundred pages, which is the result of an original eight hundred pages. The six hundred pages are there. Only you don't see them."

When you are in the revision stage, as opposed to when you are rushing through a first draft to complete it start to finish, speed is the enemy of quality. To be sure the work is the finest it can be, take your time. Columnist James Kilpatrick wrote, **"Edit your copy, then edit it again; then edit it once more.** This is the hand-rubbing process. No rough sandpapering can replace it." William Zinsser stresses the importance of revisions. He concludes, **"Rewriting is the essence of writing well; it's where the game is won or lost."**

Every time text is revised, it improves. Many times writers return to words they've written and are amazed at the flow and clarity. Other times the material embarrasses them. How I wish I could re-write many of the first books I had published using the skills I've learned over the years. Nearly every published author or poet I know feels this way.

Revising material is a constant process. In *On Writing Well*, William Zinsser proclaims, "Writing improves in direct ratio to the number of things we can keep out of it that shouldn't be there. Examine every word you put on paper. You'll find a surprising number that don't serve any purpose." He adds, "Most first drafts can be cut by 50% without losing any information or the author's voice."

Laurie Rosen, editor of thirty-seven bestsellers, advises novelists to follow ten basic steps while considering revisions. Among the ones she listed in *Writer's Digest* are: Revise toward a marketable length (Average novel length is between 60,000 and 100,000 words. Manuscripts exceeding 100,000 words are a tough sell); torque the power of your scenes (emphasize the purpose of the action); tease the reader forward into the next chapter; give your antagonist some depth, and dramatize, dramatize, dramatize."

Some authors or poets set page counts or deadlines for completion of revised drafts. Meeting them is an excellent form of discipline. **Setting reasonable deadlines is suggested.** No writer should create or edit when the brain is weary.

Critique

When an acceptable draft is completed, let others review it. It doesn't matter if your reviewer is a spouse, a relative, or a friend down the street.

Writers need a variety of people to provide objective opinions. Being removed from the material, reviewers can spot flaws and misinformation, and correct mistakes. They may even suggest an alternative means of telling a story.

The key is locating people not afraid to say what they think. Then, when criticism is leveled, swallow your ego and be receptive. While writing one book, a longtime friend who was an English major in college reviewed the manuscript. I cringed while perusing her comments since every page was saturated with red ink. On one page, she circled two paragraphs free of error and printed beside it, "Did you write this?" Her questioning my ability made my face turn red in anger, but I knew in some ways it was an off-hand compliment. At least I took it that way. When the book was completed, I knew I had become a better writer because of her stern comments.

Good writing requires dedication and perseverance since words are the writer's communication with the world. Only through hard work will the message be strong. For aspiring authors and poets attempting to impress literary agents and editors, good writing is their most important calling card.

I am convinced that anyone who uses terrific language and proper punctuation can become a good writer. The key is dedication to becoming a professional by learning the rules and abiding by them. There are no shortcuts, no quick and easy ways to write well, but hard work pays off. Not a day goes by that I don't learn something new about the writing process. Wisdom is gained from reading the great writers and studying how they manipulated their words into literature that has continued to be praised for years.

My reading of several classics to discover excerpts for the "Good Writing" section of this book enabled me to revisit the best wordsmiths who ever lived. This experience reminded me how wonderful it is to read superior writing filled with sensory descriptions of people, places, and things, clarity, intriguing dialogue, and storytelling. What a joy it is to be lifted into another world through fiction and poetry or educated about an important issue or a legend who made a difference in the world. There is no greater feeling and you know what it is like through reading of the great writers. Study them, study their methods, and learn from them. With practice, you too can write words that will stand the test of time.

Writing Tips Checklist

- Purchase and read grammar and punctuation books including *Elements of Style* by Professors Strunk and White.

- Avoid overuse of adverbs and adjectives. Look for nouns and verbs that stand on their own.

- Eliminate clichés.

- Be brief. Avoid run-on sentences.

- Avoid superlatives. Don't exaggerate. Let facts speak for themselves.

- Use strong, active verbs that move the story forward.

- Don't overuse obscure words to impress.

- Avoid weak words such as probably, maybe, something, anything, awhile, several, lots, a lot, almost, perhaps, and so forth.

- Construct clear, concise sentences. Don't use too many "ands."

- Attempt to use positive words and avoid "not."

- Don't use "etc." or other abbreviations.

- Write out the numbers one to ninety-nine and numbers beginning sentences, except with percentages, distances, and age.

- Avoid exclamation marks unless called for in dialogue.

- Remember the general rule that quotation marks are positioned outside periods and commas.

- Use single quotes for a quote within a quote.

- Avoid phrases such as "It is interesting that," or "I really believe that."

- Italicize book titles, magazines, CDs, films, operas, and plays; quotation marks are used for poems, short stories, articles, songs, and book chapters.

Manuscript Techniques
Format Do's and Don'ts

Do use 8 ½ x 11—20 pound, unlined bond paper.

Do use black type.

Do use Times New Roman print.

Do type on one side of the paper.

Do use a one-inch margin on the left side of the paper.

Do set at least a one-inch margin on the right side of the paper.

Don't staple the pages together.

Do double-space the lines utilizing 12 point font.

Don't underline book titles, chapter titles, and hyperlinks

Do average 250 words per page—(twenty-five, sixty character lines).

Do indent and single-space lengthy quotes or excerpts.

Don't use quotation marks when indenting quotes or excerpts.

Do provide chapter titles and sub-titles using 18- and 16- point font size, respectively.

Do center chapter titles and subtitles.

Don't leave subheadings at the bottom of a page.

Don't provide personal contact information on cover page.

Do include address, telephone number, fax, and e-mail information in query letter.

Optional—Type first word of your last name and keyword from title at left margin on each page.

Do type page number in lower right hand corner of page.

Do provide running number of pages in lower right hand corner of page.

Do check to make certain no pages are left out.

Don't submit manuscript until it has been edited several times. Perfection is required.

Don't trust your computer to do the work for you—check the dictionary.

Don't type "The End" on the final page of the manuscript.

Do reduce illustrations or photographs to 8 ½ x 11 paper if they exceed that size.

Do print, if at all possible, on a laser printer.

Poetry Submissions

Do use same preparation suggestions as above with the below - mentioned additions.

Don't type more than one poem to a page.

Do single-space the text.

Do leave two spaces between stanzas.

Don't include personal contact information on each page.

Do include above information in query letter.

Do begin title of poem four or five lines from top of each page.

Do center title of poem.

Do type title of poem in all caps.

Do leave three spaces between title of poem and first line of poem.

Appendix

Learning From Others

Writing Samples

There is no doubt that your writing will improve each time you write—but if and only if you continue to learn. Reading good writing is essential to achieve this goal since we can learn so much from those who have become successful authors and poets. By reading their selected works, you will see that they have mastered the art of storytelling through the use of strong, visual words providing excellent pacing and a sense of drama.

As you read the text and lines of poetry included, note the tone of the writing, the voice, and most important, the excellent use of grammar and punctuation. I often suggest in our "How To Become A Published Author or Poet: A to Z" seminars that writers read good writing before they begin to write. Through osmosis, the good writing creeps into the writer's brain and provides inspiration and ideas that improve the text whether it is fiction, non-fiction, or poetry.

By presenting a wide variety of writing, I trust you will discover authors and poets who write in the genre you have chosen for your work. There is also a reading list provided after the excerpts to guide you to additional books that are excellent resources.

When you read the following text, you will note that many of the published writers have broken rules suggested in this book. Many times their having done so is based on the style of the writer, but be careful not to emulate the mistakes made. Style is one thing, but persistent use of bad grammar and punctuation is a death knell for aspiring authors and poets. Learn from the good writing and avoid the bad.

Fiction

Anthony Burgess

A Clockwork Orange

The chelloveck sitting next to me, there being this long big plushy seat that ran round three walls, was well away with his glazzies glazed and sort of burbling slovos like 'Aristotle wishy washy works outing cyclamen get forfiulate smartish.' He was in the land all right, well away, in orbit, and I knew what it was like, having tried it like everybody else had done, but at this time I'd got to thinking it was a cowardly sort of a veshch, O my brothers. You'd lay there after you'd drunk the old moloko and then you got the messel that everything all round you was sort of in the past. You could viddy it all right, all of it, very clear – tables, the stereo, the lights, the sharps and the malchicks – but it was like some veshch that used to be there but was not there not no more. And you were sort of hypnotized by your boot or shoe or a finger-nail as it might be, and at the same time you were sort of picked up by the old scruff and shook like it might be a cat. You got shook and shook till there was nothing left.

Note: This example has a completely new language integrated into the text with English. Nadsat is a Russian-based language Burgess created for the text and replaces words like "man" with "chelloveck" and so forth. This is a great example of Burgess's mastery of the English language and his ability to manipulate it.

Mary Higgins Clark

Daddy's Little Girl

"Have you had any response to that sign you carried outside Sing Sing?"

"As a matter of fact, I have," I said, giving him what Peter Lawlor calls my mysterious self-satisfied smile.

He frowned. I had piqued his curiosity, which is exactly what I wanted to do. "It's all over town that you had some pretty nasty things to say to Rob Westerfield at the Parkinson Inn today."

"There's no law against being honest and there's certainly not one that says you have to make nice with murderers."

The Second Time Around

"When I met Dr. Kendall last week, I had thought of her as not being particularly attractive, but now when she looked directly at me, I realized that there was a compelling, almost smoldering fire that had not then been apparent to me. I had noticed her determined chin, but her dark blunt-cut hair had been tucked between her ears, and I had not taken in the curious shade of her grayish green eyes."

> Note: Clark's books feature terrific dialogue through character interaction. We learn about them through what they say instead of excessive description.

Sue Grafton

M Is For Malice

"The run itself was unsatisfactory. The dawn was overcast, the sky a brooding gray unrelieved by any visible sunrise. Gradually, daylight overtook the lowering dark, but the whole lot of it had the bleached look of an old black-and-white photograph."

> Note: Word usage sets the mood, gives readers a sense of what the scene looks like.

John Grisham

The Firm

"They left Chickasaw Gardens and drove west with the traffic toward downtown, into the fading sun. They held hands, but said little. Mitch opened the sun roof and rolled down the windows. Abby picked through a box of old cassettes and found Springsteen. The stereo worked fine. 'Hungry Heart' blew from the windows as the little shiny roadster made its way toward the river."

"The warm sticky, humid Memphis summer air settled in with the dark. Softball fields came to life as teams of fat men with tight polyester pants and lime-green and fluorescent –shirts laid chalk lines and prepared to do battle. Cars full of teenagers crowded into fast food joints to drink beer and gossip and check out the opposite sex."

> Note: Grisham's writing style provides the essentials to push the story Forward. He is criticized for not providing detail and depth,

but this best-selling author knows modern-day readers don't want to be bogged down with needless facts.

Graham Greene

The Ministry of Fear

"There are dreams which belong only partly to the unconscious; these are the dreams we remember on waking so vividly that we deliberately continue them, and so fall asleep again and wake and sleep and then dream goes on without interruption, with a thread of logic the pure dream doesn't possess.

Rowe was exhausted and frightened; he had made tracks half across London while the nightly raid got under way. It was an empty London with only occasional bursts of noise and activity. An umbrella shop was burning at the corner of Oxford Street; in Wardour Street he walked through a cloud of grit: a man with a grey dusty face leant against a wall and laughed and a warden said sharply, 'That's enough now. It's nothing to laugh about.' None of these things mattered. They were like something written; they didn't belong to his own life and he paid them no attention. But he had to find a bed, and so somewhere south of the river he obeyed Hilfe's advice and at last went underground."

Note: Watch the pacing, how Greene moves the story along with nary a word wasted.

Ernest Hemingway

The Old Man and the Sea

"He could not see the green of the shore now but only the tops of the blue hills that showed white as though they were snow-capped and the clouds that looked like high snow mountains above them. The sea was very dark and the light made prisms in the water. The myriad flecks of the plankton were annulled now by the high sun and it was only the great deep prisms in the blue water that the old man saw now with his lines going straight down into the water that was a mile deep."

Note: good example of visual writing – notice how Hemingway makes readers feel like they are right in the boat with the fisherman.

A Moveable Feast

"Sylvia had a lively, sharply sculptured face, brown eyes that were as alive as small animals and as gay as a young girl's, and wavy brown hair that was brushed back from her fine forehead and cut thick below her ears and at the line of the collar of the brown velvet jacket she wore. She had pretty legs and she was kind, cheerful and interested, and loved to make jokes and gossip. No one that I ever knew was nicer to me."

Note: Hemingway breaks the rules with a run-on sentence, but his description is powerful. Use of "that" in the final sentence could be avoided.

Greg Isles

Sleep No More

"Looking up, he saw Eve Sumner standing at the top of the stairs. Gone were the navy skirt suit and heels. She wore a bright yellow sundress that looked like something a St. Croix islander might wear. Her feet were bare, and her hair was tied back with a ruby scarf, exposing her fine neck."

"His arms and legs felt shaky, as thought he couldn't trust them. Memories of his last hour with Eve flashed through his mind like flares in the darkness, blanking out his thoughts. She came to him, like quick cuts in a film."

Note: Good use of metaphor in the final sentence provides clear picture of action. Notice correct punctuation usage with dialogue, especially positioning of period inside quotation marks.

James Joyce

The Portrait of an Artist As A Young Man

"O how cold and strange it was to think of that! All the dark was cold and strange. There were pale strange faces there, great eyes like carriage lamps. They were the ghosts of murderers, the figures of marshals who had received their death

wounds on battlefields far away over the sea. What did they wish to say that their faces were so strange?"

The Dead from *The Dubliners*

"An old man was dozing in a great hooded chair in the hall. He lit a candle in the office and went before them to the stairs. They followed him in silence, their feet falling in soft thuds on the thickly carpeted stairs. She mounted the stairs behind the porter, her head bowed in the ascent, her frail shoulders curved with a burden, her skirt girt tightly about her."

> Note: Joyce was the master of description. Note the use of adjectives has a nice balance to it. The phrase "her frail shoulders curved with a burden" nails the appearance of the character.

Jack Kerouac

On the Road

"Everybody was rocking and roaring. Galatea and Marie with beers in their hands were standing on their chairs, shaking and jumping. Groups of colored guys stumbled in from the street, falling over one another to get there. 'Stay with it, man!' roared a man with a foghorn voice, and he let out a big groan that must have been heard clear out in Sacramento, ah'haa!"

"We drove on. Across the immense plain of night lay the first Texas town, Dalhart, which I'd crossed in 1947. It lay glimmering on the dark floor of the earth, fifty miles away. The land by moonlight was all mesquite and wastes. On the horizon was the moon. She fattened, she grew huge and rusty, she mellowed and rolled, till the morning star contended and dews began to blow in our winds – and we rolled."

Note: Kerouac's writing makes readers feel like they are in the car with him as he travels across America. Note the terrific description of the moon.

Harper Lee

To Kill A Mockingbird

"Scout," said Atticus, "nigger-lover is just one of those terms that don't mean anything – like snot-nose. It's hard to explain – ignorant, trashy people use it when they think somebody's favoring Negroes over and above themselves. It's slipped into usage with some people like ourselves, when they want a common, ugly term to label somebody."

Note: Lee's vivid language is powerful and drives his story. Clarity is apparent, Lee never minced words.

Jack London

Call of the Wild

"It was only an old and battered harmonica, tenderly treasured and patiently repaired; but it was the best that money could buy, and out of its silver reeds he drew weird, vagrant airs which men had never heard before. Then the dog, dumb of throat, with teeth tight-clenched, would back away, inch by inch, to the farthest cabin corner."

Note: London's writing makes the reader almost hear the tone of the harmonica being played. And see the dog retreat to a corner in protest.

Terry McMillan

How Stella Got Her Groove Back

"I try my damnedest to wipe the smirk off my face and say, 'Nothing. And your check's on the kitchen counter. Go get it."

"You didn't go down there and fall in love with a twenty-one-year old, did you Stella?"

"Are you crazy?"

"No. *I'm* not crazy. Are you? And she is staring at me like she hasn't seen me in twenty years or like I've just cut off all my hair or dyed it some outrageous color and she is giving me a serious make-over. "Something is different about you Stella, and Ima tell you something. You look better now than I've seen you look in a long time. I'm not kidding, you actually have like a twinkle or something in your damn eye."

> Note: Excitement prevails through word usage and the tone of the writing. The story being conveyed is topped off with the descriptive words "you actually have a twinkle or something in your damn eye."

Larry McMurtry

Dead Man's Walk

"We could run for them hills – shoot our way through," he said. "I doubt that five or six of us would make it. We'd give the man scrap, at least, if we did that."

"Not a one of us would make it," Bigfoot said. "Of course, they might spare Matilda."

"I don't want to be spared if Shad ain't," Matilda said.

"You're a big target, Matty," Bigfoot observed in a kindly tone. "They might shoot you before they even realized you were female."

> Note: Good example of exciting dialogue between characters. Crisp language brings the story alive.

Herman Melville

Moby Dick

"In the midst of the consternation, Queerqueg dropped deftly to his knees and crawling under the path of the boom, whipped hold of a rope, secured one end to the bulwarks, and then flinging the other like a lasso, caught it round the boom as it swept over his head, and at the next jerk, the spar was that way trapped, and all was safe. The schooner was run into the wind, and while the hands were clearing away

the stern boat, Queequeg , stripped to the waist, darted from side to side with a long living arc of a leap."

> Note: Melville's text produces a film-like image for readers as to what is occurring on the ship. We can almost hear the waves splashing, threatening the ship's very being.

Jacquelyn Mitchard

The Deep End of the Ocean

"But Candy knew, as everyone knew, as Beth knew, that the whole legal process would turn out to be mostly theater, an elaborate pantomime intended for no purpose but competition, like binding up the newspaper corner to corner, with twine and setting them at the curb. All the hearing would accomplish, Candy predicted, would be to provide a public witnessing of tying that knot, securing it, snipping the cord."

> Note: Use of the metaphor is effective, but not overdone. Readers understand the message, the clear meaning of the author's words.

Margaret Mitchell

Gone With The Wind

"Scarlett, Melanie, and Ms. Pittypat sat in front of the *Daily Examiner* office in the carriage with the top back, sheltered beneath their parasols. Scarlett's hands shook so that her parasol wobbled above her head. Pitty was so excited her nose quivered in her round face like a rabbits, but Melanie sat as though carved of stone, her dark eyes growing darker and darker as time went by."

> Note: The use of the metaphor describing the nose quivering is effective. Great example of "showing" readers what is occurring instead of "telling" them.

James A. Michener

Centennial

"They form a strange pair, this short, stocky Frenchman and this slim red-bearded Scot. Each taciturn when on the prairie, neither pried into the affairs of the other. Without commenting on the fact, McKeag had now heard Pasquinel tell others that his wife was in Montreal, Detroit, and New Orleans, and he began to suspect there was none."

> Note: The writing provides good character description and a sense of drama. This paragraph has a complete beginning, middle, and end.

Joyce Carol Oates

We Were The Mulvaneys

"There was the Mulvaney cork bulletin board on the wall. Festooned with color snapshots, clippings, blue and red ribbons, Dad's Chamber of Commerce 'medal,' dried wallflowers, gorgeous seed-catalog pictures of tomatoes, snapdragons, columbine. Beneath what were visible were more items, and beneath those probably more. Like archeological strata. A recent history of the Mulvaneys."

Note: visual words are used to set a scene. The bulletin board comes alive. Use of the verb "Festooned" is original and clever.

George Orwell

Down and Out in Paris and London

"My hotel was called the Hotel des Trois Moineaux. It was a dark, rickety warren of five stories, cut up by wooden partitions into forty rooms. The rooms were small and inveterately dirty, for there was no maid, and Madame F., the *patronne*, had no time to do any sweeping. The walls were as thin as matchwood,

and to hide the cracks they had been covered with layer after layer of pink paper, which had come loose and housed innumerable bugs. Near the ceiling long lines of bugs marched all day like columns of soldiers . . ."

"Charlie was a youth of family and education, who had run away from home and lived on occasional remittances. Picture him very pink and young, with the fresh cheeks and soft brown hair of a nice little boy, and lips excessively red and wet, like cherries. His feet are tiny, his arms abnormally short, his hands dimpled like a baby's. He has a way of dancing and capering while he talks, as though he were too happy and too full of life to keep still for an instant."

"The room had a dirty, mixed smell of food and sweat. Everywhere in the cupboards, behind the piles of crockery, were squalid stores of food that the waiters had stolen. There were only two sinks, and no washing basin, and it was nothing unusual for a waiter to wash his face in the water in which clean crockery was rinsing. But the customers saw nothing of this. There were a coco-nut mat and a mirror outside the dining room door, and the waiters used to preen themselves up and go in looking the picture of cleanliness."

Note: Orwell uses visual words to captivate readers into the story. Notice how he uses the five senses to bring the characters alive. Readers find themselves drawn in with the story, thinking "I'm glad I never ate at this restaurant."

James Patterson

Suzanne's Diary for Nicholas

"They went to bed for the first time on that rainy night, and he made her notice the music of the raindrops as they fell on her street, the rooftop, and even the trees outside her apartment. It was beautiful, it was music, but soon they had forgotten the patter of the rain, and everything else, except for the urgent touch of each other."

Note: A simple, touching use of words to describe passion. Instead of flinging body parts around and providing heavy breathing, the author presents us with a touching portrayal of two people who are in love.

Anna Quindlen

Blessings

"Mount Mason had seemed dusty, too dusty, and out of date, aging the way that the cheap houses around the industrial park did, peeling, cracked, disintegrating, instead of mellowing. So many of her landmarks had gone, the old limestone bank building chopped up into a travel agency, a beauty parlor, a used bookstore, the boxy brick hardware store refaced with some horrid imitation stone and made into a place that sold records."

Note: The author uses effective, visual words to describe a slice of history. The use of "some horrid imitation stone" is the perfect way for the author to make a point.

Ayn Rand

Atlas Shrugged

"She glanced at him with the faint suggestion of a smile, thinking of how often she had said these words to him and of the desperate bravery with which he was now trying to tell her: Don't worry. He caught her glance, he understood, and the answering hint of his smile had a touch of embarrassing apology."

> Note: The author uses a minimum of words to describe the emotion present between the characters. Other authors might need several paragraphs to give us the tone of the moment, but Rand ties it up with key words that leave no doubt as to what is occurring.

Anne Rice

Interview With The Vampire

"I held fast to Claudia, ready in an instant to shove her behind me, to step forward to meet him. But then I saw with astonishment that his eyes did not see me as I saw him and he was trudging under the weight of the body he carried toward the monastery door. The moon fell now on his bowed head, on a mass of black wavy hair that touched his bent shoulder, on the full black sleeve of his coat."

> Note: Terrific description provides exactly what readers need to know about what the character feels while approaching the man. "The moon fell now on his bowed head" provides an effective description.

Tom Robbins

Villa Incognito

"Sure, as catalogued earlier, he had his charm and wiles, attractions that survived the metamorphosis from beast to man, and there were high-bred city women for whom his backwards manners were actually a kind of turn-on, a thrilling intrusion of the rustic over the overly refined."

"Let me pour you some bubbly, baby. I want to hear your news on America. Obviously, the ol' homeland is still hiding behind its mask of lipstick democracy and mascara faith, but what bouncy enterprising weirdness is leaking out around the edges of its disguises? *That's* the real America. That's what defines its existence."

Note: Robbins' language is rich with meaning. Notice how he makes his point regarding feelings about America.

Salman Rushdie

Haroun and the Sea of Stories

"As Haroun passed through the huge doors of P2C2E House, his heart sank. He stood in the vast, echoing entrance hall as white-coated Eggheads walked rapidly past him in every direction. Haroun fancied that they all eyed him with a mixture of anger, contempt, and pity. He had to ask three Eggheads the way to the Walrus's office before he finally found it, after many mazy wanderings around P2C2E House that reminded him of following Blabbermouth around the palace. At last, however, he was standing in front of a golden door on which were written the words: GRAND COMPTROLLER OF PROCESSES TOO COMPLICATED TO EXPLAIN. I.M.D. WALRUS, ESQUIRE. KNOCK AND WAIT."

Note: Terrific description; great name selection. Readers can imagine themselves right into the thick of this story.

J. D. Salinger

The Catcher In The Rye

"It wasn't snowing out any more, but every once in a while you could hear a car somewhere not being able to get started. You could also hear old Ackley snoring. Right through the goddam shower curtains you could hear him. He had sinus trouble and he couldn't breathe too hot when he was asleep. That guy had just about everything – sinus trouble, pimples, lousy teeth, halitosis, crummy fingernails. You have to feel a little sorry for the crazy sunuvabitch"

Note: Salinger sets the stage for our sense of hearing with perfect language. The descriptions of Ackley make readers feel like they know him.

Dai Sijie

Balzac and the Little Chinese Seamstress

"The branches whistled through the air as they swung, one after another. The blows left livid weals on Luo's flesh but my friend underwent the flogging impassively. Although he was conscious, it was as though he were in a dream where it was all happening to someone else. I couldn't tell what he was thinking, but I was very anxious, and the remark he had made in the mine shaft a few weeks before came back to me, reverberating in the cruel whoosh of the branches; 'I've had this idea stuck in my head; that I'm going to die in this mine.'"

"The room served as shop, workplace and dining room all at once. The floorboards were grimy and streaked with yellow-and-black gobs of dried spittle left by clients. You could tell they were not washed down daily. There were hangers with finished garments suspended on a string across the middle of the room. The corners were piled high with bolts of material and folded clothes, which were under siege from an army of ants."

Note: Sijie's locations come alive through strong images. Readers are transported into the room where the seamstress works. Use of "under siege from an army of ants" is superb word usage.

John Steinbeck

In Dubious Battle

"Look, Jim, I want to give you a picture of what it's like to be a Party member. You'll get a chance to vote on every decision, but once the vote's in, you'll have to obey. When we have money we try to give field workers twenty dollars a month to eat on. I don't remember a time when we ever had the money. Now listen to the work: In the field you'll have to work alongside the men, and you'll have to do the Party work after that, sometimes sixteen, eighteen hours a day. You'll have to get your food where you can. Do you think you could do that?"

"Yes."

Nilson touched the desk here and there with his fingertips. "Even the people you're trying to help will hate you most of the time. Do you know that?"

"Yes."

"Well, why do you want to join, then?"

Jim's grey eyes half closed in perplexity. At last he said, "In the jail there were some Party men. They talked to me. Everything's been a mess, all my life. Their lives weren't messes. They were working toward something. I want to work toward something. I feel dead. I thought I might get alive again."

Of Mice and Men

"It was Sunday afternoon. The resting horses nibbled the remaining wisps of hay, and they stamped their feet and they bit the wood of the mangers and rattled the halter chains. The afternoon sun sliced in through the cracks of the barn walls and lay in bright lines on the hay. There was the buzz of flies in the air, the lazy afternoon humming."

Tortilla Flat

"When the beans are ripe, the little bushes are pulled and gathered into piles, to dry crisp for the threshers. Then is the time to pray that the rain may hold off. When the little piles of beans lie in lines, yellow against the dark fields, you will see the farmers watching the sky, scowling with dread at every cloud that sails over; for if a rain comes, the bean piles must be turned over to dry again."

> Note: Steinbeck is the master of storytelling. Watch the pacing of the writing, the drama, how the author provides visual images certain to keep the reader's attention. Use of verbs such as "nibbled," "stamped," and "rattled" bring the text alive.

Hunter S. Thompson

Kingdom of Fear

"So the following night I took the little auto that I'd bought with me to Rio, a cheap automatic. I carried it all over South America, usually loaded. Why carry one that's not? I tied it around my neck with a string—it was too hot to carry anywhere else."

"A shudder ran through me, but I gripped the wheel and stared straight ahead, ignoring this sudden horrible freak show in my car. I lit a cigarette, but I was not calm. Sounds of sobbing and the ripping of cloth came from the backseat. The man they called Judge had straightened himself out and was now resting easily in the front seat, letting out long breaths of air . . ."

> Note: Thompson's flair for the dramatic is his trademark, but his word usage is captivating. The use of "sudden horrible freak show in my car" provides exactly the image he seeks.

Scott Turow

Presumed Innocent

"Carolyn, for her part, was chilling in her command. The weekend after our initial night together, I spent hours – dazed, unrooted hours – pondering our next encounter. I had no idea what was to follow. At the door to her apartment, she had kissed my hand and said simply, 'See you.' For me, there was no thought of resistance. I would take whatever was allowed."

"Around the office, Tommy Molto was nicknamed the Mad Monk. He is a former seminarian; five feet six inches if he is lucky, forty or fifty pounds overweight, badly pockmarked, nails bitten to the quick. A driven personality. The kind to stay up all night working on a brief, to take three months without taking off a weekend. A capable attorney, but he is burdened by a zealot's poverty of judgment."

> Note: Turow is quite apt at naming characters, and describing them so readers can visualize their look, characteristics, and outlook on life. Use of "burdened by a zealot's poverty of judgment" provides a character portrayal essential to the story being told.

Virginia Woolf

Mrs. Dalloway

"You served with great distinction in the War?"

The patient repeated the word "war" interrogatively.

He was attaching meanings to words of a symbolical kind. A serious symptom, to be noted on the card.

"The War?" the patient asked. The European War—that little shindy of schoolboys and gunpowder? Had he served with distinction? He really forgot. In the War itself he had failed.

"Yes, he served with the greatest distinction," Rezia assured the doctor; "he was promoted."

"And they have the very highest opinion of you at your office?" Sir William murmured, glancing at Mr. Brewer's very generously worded letter. "So that you have nothing to worry you, no financial anxiety, nothing?"

He had committed an appalling crime and been condemned to death by human nature.

"I have-I have," he began, "committed a crime-"

"He has done nothing wrong whatever," Rezia assured the doctor. If Mr. Smith would wait, said Sir William, he would speak to Mrs. Smith in the next room. Her husband was very seriously ill, Sir William said. Did he threaten to kill himself?

> Note: Compelling dialogue, terrific word usage. Note the correct use of punctuation with the dialogue.

Non-Fiction

H. W. Brands

The First American – The Life and Times of Benjamin Franklin

"[Franklin] made numerous observations of the finned fish of the Atlantic. Most striking were the flying fish and the dolphins (the gilled kind, not the mammals). The reason the flying fish took to the air was to escape the dolphins, which raced beneath them, ready to gobble them up as soon as they touched down. Franklin confirmed this by noting that whenever dolphins were caught by persons on the ship – they invariably had flying fish in their bellies."

> Note: Good sentence structure. Notice that this paragraph is complete - good beginning, middle, and end.

Richard Ben Cramer

Joe DiMaggio

"It would not be a happy summer for either of the Yankees' big stories. Mantle got to the grand Bronx ball yard, took a look at the towering tiers of seats, the monuments to Huggins, Gehrig, Ruth, in the vastness of center field, the pennants and World Series flags fluttering in rows atop the scalloped balustrade . . . and he stopped hitting atomic home runs. In fact, he was trying so hard to crush the ball, to be the miracle advertised, to hit as he believed a New York Yankee must hit (harder, surely, than *he'd* ever hit) . . . he couldn't hit a thing."

> Note: Good description of Yankee Stadium – readers feel like they are right there with DiMaggio and experiencing his emotions.

Laura Hillenbrand

Seabiscuit

"Even the jaded horsemen would take a respite from their labors to see [Seabiscuit], eating their breakfasts outdoors on the benches near the siding. To joyful applause and popping flashbulbs, the horse would draw up in his railcar. He would step from his three-foot deep bed of straw, give Smith an affectionate bump with his nose and leave the train bucking."

"Spectators murmured among themselves at Smith's homemade bell. They watched quizzically as Smith lined up his horse, stepped behind him, and hit the bell, sending Seabiscuit into a rock start. Woolf hustled him deftly; having begun his career booting horses through walk-up match races in Indian country, he knew how to hit the gas on a horse."

> Note – The author uses terrific language to show what is occurring instead of telling us what is happening. Show and don't tell to make your writing more effective.

Barbara Kingsolver

Seeing Scarlet

"Then a bend in the road revealed a tiny adobe school, its bare dirt yard buzzing with activity. The Escuela del Sol Feliz took us by surprise in such a remote place, though in Costa Rica, where children matter more than the army, the sturdiest shoes are made in small sizes, and every tiny hamlet has at least a one-room school. This one had turned its charges outdoors for the day in their white and navy uniforms so the schoolyard seemed to wave with nautical flags."

> Note: Good word usage provides excellent descriptions. Note the strong adjectives used to add zest to the story.

Jon Meacham

Franklin and Winston

"To meet Roosevelt the president, 'with all his buoyant sparkle, his iridescence,' Churchill once said, was like 'opening a bottle of champagne.'"

> Note: terrific use of the language to pinpoint a strong characterization of President Roosevelt.

"Roosevelt was about to say something else when suddenly, in the flick of an eye, he turned green and great drops of sweat began to bead off his face; he put a shaky hand to his forehead," Bohlen recalled. "We were all caught by surprise."

> Note: The pacing of the writing is terrific. Action – "Roosevelt is about to speak," drama – "suddenly, in the flick of an eye," more action – "he turned green and great drops of sweat began to bead off his face," more action – "he put a shaky hand to his forehead," and finally reaction "We were all caught by surprise."

Sylvia Nastar

A Beautiful Mind

"When Eleanor irritated him with her complaints, Nash would needle her. He called her stupid and ignorant. He made fun of her pronunciation. He reminded her that she was five years older. Mostly, however, he made fun of her desire to marry him. An MIT professor, he would say, needed a woman who was his intellectual equal. 'He was always putting me down,' she recalled. 'He was always making me feel inferior.'"

> Note: Use of words like "irritated," and "needle" provide fresh meaning for the text. Also notice the correct punctuation regarding the quote used with the quotation marks outside the comma and period.

Marina Picasso

Picasso, My Grandfather

"I feel the sting of the banderilleros' barbs. I wish the film could be run backwards, so the bull would recover all his glory; the bloody lances soiling his coat would disappear as well as the barbs planted on his neck. I wish the barrera and the steps would vanish into thin air, and that a strong gust of wind would blow away the toreros and their idolatrous public. I wish the bull could be back in his field with his herd. I wish this bullfight had never been."

> Note: Good example of first person writing. Also the paragraph builds with drama as the writer creates the mood and the message intended.

"Two inseparable creatures, like birds who can only live in couples, Pablito and I bound to each other, hand in hand, forehead against forehead. We refuse to take pare in the ignominy of men."

"We hear 'ole' and strident whistling. We are paralyzed with anguish as if brimstone were about to descend from the sky. 'Do you think he will suffer?' whispers Pablito."

> Note: Good use of simile regarding the closeness of the two characters.

Emile Zola

The Dreyfus Affair

"In Paris, the all-conquering truth was on the march, and we know how the predictable storm eventually burst. M. Matthew Dreyfus denounced Major Esterhazy as the real author of the bordereau just as M. Scheurer-Kestner was about to place in the hands of the Minister of Justice a request for a revision of the Dreyfus trial. And this is where Major Esterhazy appears. Witnesses state that first he panicked; he was on the verge of suicide or about to flee. Then suddenly he became boldness itself and grew so violent that all Paris was astonished."

Note: The dramatics presented set the tone for the paragraph. The last sentence is very powerful, providing the sense of history.

Poetry

Dante Alighieri

***Inferno* (Excerpt)**

CANTO I

One night, when half my life behind me lay,
I wandered from the straight lost path afar.
Through the great dark was no releasing way;
Above that dark was no relieving star.
If yet that terrored night I think or say,
As death's cold hands its fears resuming are.

Gladly the dreads I felt, too dire to tell,
The hopeless, pathless, lightless hours forgot,
I turn my tale to that which next befell,
When the dawn opened, and the night was not.
The hollowed blackness of that waste, God wot,
Shrank, thinned, and ceased. A blinding splendour hot
Flushed the great height toward which my footsteps fell,
And though it kindled from the nether hell,
Or from the Star that all men leads, alike
It showed me where the great dawn-glories strike
The wide east, and the utmost peaks of snow.

Margaret Atwood

***Spelling* (Excerpt)**

My daughter plays on the floor
with plastic letters,
red, blue & hard yellow,
learning how to spell,
spelling,
how to make spells.

*

I wonder how many women
denied themselves daughters,
closed themselves in rooms,
drew the curtains
so they could mainline words.

*

A child is not a poem,
a poem is not a child.
There is no either / or.
However.

Elizabeth Bishop

***One Art* (Excerpt)**

The art of losing isn't hard to master;
so many things seem filled with the intent
to be lost that their loss is no disaster.

Lose something every day. Accept the fluster
of lost door keys, the hour badly spent.
The art of losing isn't hard to master.

Then practice losing farther, losing faster:
places, and names, and where it was you meant
to travel. None of these will bring disaster.

I lost my mother's watch. And look! my last, or
next-to-last, of three loved houses went.
The art of losing isn't hard to master.

William Blake

The Sick Rose
O Rose thou art sick.
The invisible worm
That flies in the night
In the howling storm:

Has found out thy bed
Of crimson joy:
And his dark secret love
Does thy life destroy.

Gwendolyn Brooks

We Real Cool

We real cool. We

Left School. We

Lurk late. We
Strike straight. We

Sing sin. We
Thin gin. We

Jazz June. We
Die soon.

Billy Collins

I Go Back into the House For a Book (Excerpt)

I turn around on the gravel
and go back to the house for a book,
something to read at the doctor's office,
and while I am inside, running the finger
of inquisition along a shelf,
another me that did not bother
to go back to the house for a book
heads out on his own,
rolls down the driveway,
and swings left toward town,
a ghost in his ghost car,
another knot in the string of time,
a good three minutes ahead of me —
a spacing that will now continue
for the rest of my life.

e.e. cummings

1(a... (a leaf falls on loneliness)

1(a

le
af
fa
ll

s)
one
l
iness

Emily Dickinson

Ah, Moon—and Star!

240

Ah, Moon—and Star!
You are very far—
But were no one
Farther than you—
Do you think I'd stop
For a Firmament—
Or a Cubit—or so?

I could borrow a Bonnet
Of the Lark—

And a Chamois' Silver Boot—
And a stirrup of an Antelope—
And be with you—Tonight!

But, Moon, and Star,
Though you're very far—
There is one—farther than you—
He—is more than a firmament—from Me—
So I can never go

Carolyn Forché

The Vistor (Excerpt)

In Spanish he whispers there is no time left.
It is the sound of scythes arcing in wheat,
the ache of some field song in Salvador.
The wind along the prison, cautious
as Francisco's hands on the inside, touching
the walls as he walks, it is his wife's breath
slipping into his cell each night while he
imagines his hand to be hers. It is a small country.

There is nothing one man will not do to another.

Robert Frost

The Pasture from *The Road Not Taken* (Excerpt)

I'm going to clean the pasture spring;

I'll only stop to rake the leaves away
(And wait to watch the water clear, I may):
I sha'nt be gone long. – You come too.

I'm going to fetch the little calf.
That's standing by the mother. It's so young.
It totters when she licks it with her tongue.
I sha'nt be gone long. You come too.

Pablo Neruda

Poetry (Excerpt)

And it was at that age...Poetry arrived
in search of me. I don't know, I don't know where
it came from, from winter or a river.
I don't know how or when,
no, they were not voices, they were not
words, nor silence,
but from a street I was summoned,
from the branches of night,
abruptly from the others,
among violent fires
or returning alone,
there I was without a face
and it touched me.

I did not know what to say, my mouth
had no way

Walt Whitman

Song of Myself (excerpt)

I celebrate myself, and sing myself,
And what I assume you shall assume,
For every atom belonging to me as good belongs to you.

I loafe and invite my soul,
I lean and loafe at my ease observing a spear of summer grass.

My tongue, every atom of my blood, form'd from this soil, this air,
Born here of parents born here from parents the same, and their
parents the same,
I, now thirty-seven years old in perfect health begin,
Hoping to cease not till death.

Creeds and schools in abeyance,
Retiring back a while sufficed at what they are, but never forgotten,
I harbor for good or bad, I permit to speak at every hazard,
Nature without check with original energy.

Sample Manuscript Text

Following are excerpts from a fiction and a non-fiction manuscript. While reading them, note the storytelling sequence, focus on detail and clarity, emphasis on word usage and description to provide visualization, and proper use of punctuation and grammar. Remember: every sentence, paragraph, and chapter has a good beginning, middle, and end.

Fiction

No Peace for The Wicked

A Sordid Tale of Injustice in Redding County

Prologue

"Get your stuff, retardo. You're going home."

The moon-faced matron stuffed a deck of cards into her denim shirt pocket, shoved her puffy hand through the Redding County jail cell door, and tossed in a folded garbage bag. It floated to the concrete floor in front of Ike Fellows's bunk.

Ike looked up, confused by the abrupt intrusion. Alice Porkman stood there sneering, one hand twirling a set of keys and the other lodged in the folds of her thick waist.

"Had to interrupt a game of cards to deal with your no good ass," Alice said. "Waste of my damn time."

Ike was lying on his bunk, dreading the moment when he would be called out for a shower. Though his long brown hair was dull and stringy, and his body odor offensive even to him, he pretended to be asleep to avoid going since showering brought back memories of Armington State Prison. Bad memories.

Her voice rising an octave, Alice repeated her words. "Ya hear me, retardo? I said pack up your shit. You're goin' home."

His keeper had used this ploy to trick him before, but having no choice, Ike, whose patchy beard and missing front teeth made him appear older than his thirty-five years, hurriedly gathered up the photo-booth picture of his sister and her kids. As Alice scraped her keys across the metal cell bars, he stuffed the photograph in the bag with his extra set of prison clothes and a wooden cross a child molester had whittled for him.

As an air raid siren cut the silence, Ike tried to move quickly. He heard the clank of the cell door key against the lock, but his hands were shaking, his movements clumsy. Alice opened the door and he obediently shuffled down the corridor, two steps behind his guardian, sucking in the smell of disinfectant spread in the cell block earlier that morning.

At a desk just beyond the cell block, Alice grabbed a clipboard. She shoved a pen in Ike's face, pointing to a space on the paper.

"Sign," she ordered, her voice dull and cold.

Ike grabbed the pen, laboriously inking his mark on the line as the foul odor of the nearby latrine lingered in the air. Alice yanked the pen away, gripped his right shoulder and shoved him toward the back door. She opened it with her free hand and pushed him out onto the wooden back steps of the jail as the door thumped closed behind him.

The fading rays of the late summer sun dipped beyond the landscape as Ike stood in the shadow of the jail, gathering the confidence to walk away. He followed the sun's descent with his wary eyes before focusing on a chirping Bob White perched on the limb of a nearby tree, then to parched red roses trailing along a neighboring fence. Across the street, he spied a worn "Bush For President" sign tacked to a pockmarked telephone pole. Beside it another read, "Manchester is G.O.P. Country."

Ike smelled the grassy scent in the thick Ohio air and tugged at the too-tight collar on his blue work shirt. For the first time in eighteen months, he could breathe without the stench of urine and mold, of unclean men in a world behind steel bars.

Ike was wearing his prison-issue jeans, the work shirt stamped with his D.O.C. number, and black, crepe-soled oxfords. The matron hadn't given him his ID or any money. Not even the $75 "gateage" inmates normally received at their release. He considered returning to ask for it, but feared being locked up again.

Ike tripped and stumbled down the jail steps. His rolling gait was the result of neurofibromatosis, Elephant Man's disease. Lumpy clusters moguled his face, hands, and arms. His shoe splayed below a pant leg cut to allow room for the huge protuberance above his left ankle. The ribbing of his dirty white cotton sock stretched tautly over the swelling.

Inmates who had come and gone during his three-week stay at the jail called him "retardo" and "one leg." When the lump festered and cracked, pus stained his sock, giving inmates more reasons to taunt him.

Though the afflicted leg slowed his pace, Ike pushed ahead, suddenly anxious to put distance between himself and the jail. With every step, he glanced over his shoulder to see if anyone was following. He trusted no one, especially policemen.

Ike walked with his head lowered, avoiding eye contact with anyone on the sidewalk and a few passing cars traveling the Manchester streets at dusk. "I gotta get to Sharon's house," he repeated as a mantra. She was his sister and only living relative.

Ike was two blocks from the jail when an unmarked, black Dodge patrol car rolled to the curb less than twenty feet from him. He quickened his step, but he couldn't out-pace the car as it crawled alongside.

The shrill sound of a familiar voice caused Ike to trip and fall. "Hey, you dumb retard," the agitator spat, his voice booming across the vacant street.

Ike didn't look, but now he was certain his release was a trick. He was going back to prison.

"Hey, retard, look at me when I talk to you," the agitator barked as Ike heard a car door slam. "You and me got some business to take care of."

Ike froze, his only possessions clutched against his chest. Tears welled. He felt helpless, sprawled on the sidewalk, afraid to move.

Seconds later, Ike felt his tormentor's presence hovering over him and the sound of handcuffs clanking in the air.

"You dogshit wimp," the voice scolded as handcuffs appeared in front of Ike's eyes. "Did you really think I was gonna let your sorry gimp ass walk around *my* town?"

Book I

Chapter One
Call for Help

To drink or not to drink, this is the question.

I, Luther Parsons, a practicing attorney and part-time television legal analyst, have a decision to make. As I watch what's left of a burnt orange ball settle behind the western most peak of the Maricopa Mountains in central Arizona, I'm clutching the neck of a full bottle of Jack Daniels in my right hand.

For nearly a half hour, I've been plastered against the reclining leather seat of my beloved Audi debating with myself, sizing up the devil. One sip of whiskey, I know, will lead to a second, and a third, and within thirty minutes, the bottle will be empty. By morning, I'll be lying in bed soaked in my own vomit, my body infiltrated with the same poison that has demonized me many times before.

I headed for the Arizona desert in a rage lasting until I crossed the muddy Mississippi. Ignoring two preliminary hearings, the sentencing of a rapist who is the worst human being on the face of the earth, and an oral argument in front of the State Supreme Court regarding a change of judge motion appealed on a whim, I marched out of the courthouse in Manchester, Ohio, climbed into the "black beast," as I call it, and headed for Interstate 70 and points west. My excuse for leaving was a town full of hypocrites who think I'm a dimwit, a law practice that has been shrinking in size ever since a client of mine named Dr. David Duval went on a rampage, a civil judgment for $350,000 against me that will more than likely trigger my filing bankruptcy, and another dragged-out fight with my partner in life, Jessie, a bombastic wisp of a woman who edges my temper into the red zone.

After what seemed like the fiftieth fight of the month, this one over accusations that yours truly was a bit too friendly with the sexy bailiff in Superior Court 4, she airmailed a bedroom lamp in my direction. It crashed into the wall, barely missing me and our blind beagle, Bob.

When morning arrived, I decided it was time for a road trip. Arizona was my old stomping grounds, a comforting place where I knew I could raise hell without someone hurling light fixtures at me.

The moment the Audi crossed the Arizona state line and I spotted a towering saguaro, my blood pressure dropped fifty points. As I passed by cacti, roadrunners, jackrabbits, and coiling rattlesnakes hissing in the 100 degree heat, I opened the sunroof and gulped new life into my lungs since a convenient memory permits me to ignore a few of the Arizona memories that still haunt me.

Four years ago, I trekked to the golden West after the legal powers-that-be in Ohio decided I needed a "sabbatical," as they dubbed it. To avoid permanent disbarment, I packed a suitcase, threw in every country music CD I owned along with my precious Fender guitar, and headed out of Manchester intent on never returning.

For eleven months, I lived on an exotic fringe, sleeping until noon and lying by the pool at a fancy apartment complex stocked with bleached blondes. Around nine, my Fender guitar and I paraded over to the redneck Diamond Bar where owner Lucy Sanchez let me play tunes with a country band I called Luther and Magic Country. We never challenged George Strait, but the locals loved us.

Once the final set was finished at 2:00 a.m., the fun really began. By then, I'd gulped down enough Jack to kill most mortals and there was always a cuddly country music groupie around who was enamored enough with my music to be enticed into a roll in the hay. Many times I woke up in places I couldn't identify. On one occasion, I found myself in a border-town hacienda where I had to fend off the shotgun-toting father of a lovely senorita. For some reason, he wasn't as captivated with my charms as his daughter was.

Heavy doses of booze hid the real world and the drunken binges continued until I finally met my match. This occurred one morning when I opened my eyes and realized something other than my tongue and teeth was occupying my mouth. After several seconds, I realized it was a big toe. Oh so carefully I removed the smelly digit while trying to remember who the attached foot and body belonged to.

Unable to extricate myself from the naked torso flopped over mine, I laid back trying to recollect the night's events. I remembered playing at Lucy's, but little else. "Shit," I blurted, loud enough that the body pinning me wiggled slightly causing the spongy toe to brush my nose.

As I pushed it to the side with my free hand (the other was buried under a leg the size of a small tree trunk), I thought back to Lucy's. I'd finished the first set. No, I hadn't. Yes, I had. No, I hadn't. I hadn't because I was so drunk that I'd fallen off the makeshift stage and into the lap of, oh no, yes it was, Beatrice, a/k/a Bee, the chubby stripper from Polly's Puff Parlor down the street with tits the size of soccer balls.

Her image triggered a recollection of a car speeding across the desert at a hundred-plus miles per hour, my hair smashed against my face. Bee, who somehow had loaded me into her powder blue '74 Caddie convertible, raced down the highway as if she and Mario Andretti were headed for the finish line. Only twice did we stop and that was to let me barf my guts out.

Our desert escapade continued with Bee whooping and hollering like a drunken cowboy after a cattle drive. I knew I was in serious trouble when we passed a state trooper. He simply waved at Bee as if she was a law abiding citizen doing twenty-five in a congested school zone.

When I saw signs announcing the Mexican border, I pleaded with Bee to find us a motel for the night. Her eyes were flashing and she ignored me, focused as she was on screaming at the moon.

As the border checkpoint drew closer, anxiety took over and I contemplated leaping out of the speeding Caddie. Bee must have sensed my mindset, and she pumped the accelerator so hard I was nearly flipped out on the pavement. "You ain't goin nowhere my sweet Luther," the Bee-woman bellowed. "You just stay here with momma."

Less than a 1000 feet from the checkpoint, Momma suddenly reversed the Caddie's course and headed deep into the desert. "I'm a gonna show you Heaven," Bee screamed as she rocketed across the scattering sand dodging cacti and deadwood. "Pure and simple, my boy," she roared, "Heaven."

As she spoke, Bee handed me the bottle of JD. I took a gulp hoping to dull the pain in my head. Bee was jabbering, paying little attention to where she was going until we sideswiped an embankment. I hit my head on the dashboard and slumped into the passenger seat, dead to the world.

I awoke spread-eagled on the front hood of the Caddie. Flashbulbs nearly blinded me as I tried to move my arms and hands, but they were bound to the rear view mirror mounts. When I bobbed my head up toward the star-lit sky, I saw that I was buck naked, my willie pointed straight up like a Saturn rocket ready to blast off.

"Okay, big boy," Bee hollered as she stepped back from the car, her hands full of Polaroids. "This is God's true Heaven. Just look at those beautiful stars."

I mumbled something about being tied up and the photographs, but Bee was on a mission. "This is it, my boy, this is Heaven, God's Heaven. This is as good as it gets. And big Bee here is gonna make you feel so good you'll never wanna leave her. Never, ever, am I right, boy?"

Before answering, my nose felt something cold and steely. It took a split second for me to realize it was the shiny barrel of a thirty eight that Bee had aimed right between my eyes. I nevertheless managed a faint, "yes" as Bee began to fire the pistol into the air while she howled at a four-legged creature who galloped across the horizon.

"Now I'm gonna put on a show for you, big boy," Bee yelped as she smacked me with a soggy kiss. "One *you* get for free."

Moments later, with Tammy Wynette's "Stand By Your Man" blaring on the radio, Bee, standing shakily on the hood above me, shed her scanty clothes. Moments later, Bee's big boobs banged against my cheeks with the force of weighted boxing gloves as an embarrassed coyote howled in the distance.

The nightmare's images with Bee suddenly fresh in my mind, I began the process of sliding out from under my captor, hoping to leave without waking her. I move Bee's meaty leg to one side, trying not to look at the hairy ass that was staring down at me. I hesitated when I heard a sigh, then continued. One of my feet touched the floor, and I eased myself away from the bed. I froze while Bee flopped over, but when her snoring resumed, I quickly scanned the room trying to figure out where the hell I was. Nearly a minute passed before I discovered a matchbook with "Starlight Motel, Snowflake, Arizona" imprinted on it.

Retrieving my jeans, Tequila Sunrise T-shirt and a pair of black and white low-cut Chuck Taylor Converse sneakers, I silently crept out of the room and down a foyer to a creaking door that led to the outside world. I slipped on my pants and shirt and ambled across the parking lot, shoes in hand.

A trucker named Zeke with a passion for Led Zeppelin took pity on me. Four hours later, I was back in the safety of my Scottsdale apartment, still shaken by the crazed encounter with Bee. I took the longest, hottest shower in the history of mankind trying to rid myself of the French perfumed scent of my kidnapper. Once I dried off, I emptied the kitchen cabinet of leftover liquor. The Lord, in the form of Bee, had spoken—it was time to go on the wagon.

Less than three hours later, I packed my belongings, settled up with the apartment owner, and headed east. Outside Denver, I called my dad and told him I was coming home. He cried and so did I.

These memories reappear as I sit in my Audi deciding whether to down the Jack Daniels. In the years that passed since my last drink, I'd become a changed man, one whose representation of Dr. David Duval led to appearances on *CNN* as a legal analyst.

Then the Duval case blew up and life turned sour. Jessie's constant bitching and the $350,000 debt I can't pay added to the mix, and I've become one of those "oh poor me" people who is certain God has forsaken them.

Remembering how bad it was with Jessie blocks out logic and I uncap the bottle of Jack, deciding the demon has won. "Screw the world," I blurt out with a forceful voice. "Screw the whole damn world."

Just as the bottle top brushes my parched lips with the biting taste of whisky, the cellular phone lying on the console buzzes. The sound startles me, and whiskey leaks down my chin onto the printed shirt I bought at Eddie Bauer. I pat it down with my left hand as the cell continues to ring. Reluctantly, I pick up the noisy device and cushion it to my ear.

Chapter Two
Sonny's Lament

"Luther Parsons, attorney at law," I answer without thinking.

"Thought you were off duty, counselor, on vacation," the familiar voice on the other end suggests.

"Forgot myself, Sonny. How the hell you doing?" I ask while loosening the eagle buckle of my western belt one notch.

Sonny Burk is the leader of the 18th Street Irregulars, a crusty band of neer-do-wells that I've snatched from the clutches of the law from time to time. The Irregulars know what's going on in Manchester, Cincinnati's bedroom community, almost before it happens. Sonny's the best. Jessie refers to him as the "walking beauty shop."

"Those sons-a-bitches. Those sons-a-bitches," Sonny, a disciple of Bruce Springsteen, exclaims, his voice rising with each syllable. "What they did to Ike and Homer, they oughta be strung up by their balls."

"Sonny, calm down," I say. "Who's Ike and who's Homer? And who in the hell is they?"

"Ike is Ike Fellows, cousin of mine. A good guy who's had it tough. He's a clubfoot. A little slow. Got those damn lumps all over his body. Homer Kendrik's slow too, but different. He's a humpback. Looks like his head comes out of his chest."

"Whoa, Sonny, you're way ahead of me," I interrupt. "What happened?"

A deep tubercular exhale on the other end of the phone line tells me Sonny's lit up. He's a four-pack-a-day man like me.

"Okay. Here's the deal. Two years ago, some dude name of Wesley Whitehall got blown away. Shotgun blast to the head. Remember?"

As Sonny speaks, I recap the JD bottle and scribble on the backside of an envelope. My half-smoked Marlboro perches precariously on the edge of the car ashtray, threatening to drop ashes on the dark gray floor mat.

"Drug case as I recall?"

"Right. Whitehall was a heavy-duty drug dealer. Connections in Columbia, Mexico, all the right places. Marijuana, coke, uppers, downers, snappers, yellows, reds, take your choice."

"Regular CVS," I say.

"The full menu," Sonny replies. "Anyway, they found him face down on Valentine's Day in a pool of blood at his apartment."

"Robbery, revenge or romance?" I ask.

"Huh?"

"Who killed him? A thief, the competition or a jealous woman?"

Sonny laughs. A hyena laugh with a sinister edge.

"None of the above. And it wasn't the butler, either."

"Who was the investigating officer, Sonny? Somebody screwed up."

"None other than Bud Hodges handled the case," he barks.

"Hodges? He's involved in this?" I yell, my voice escaping into the silent desert.

"You're there, counselor. Detective Hodges, the town's favorite son, handled the case. First, he picked up Homer Kendrik, then some juicehead named Charley Bottoms, then Ike Fellows. Bottoms had an alibi, but Homer and Ike confessed to killing Whitehall. Case closed. Wrapped up. Lickety-split."

"And then?" I ask, uncapping the Jack Daniels bottle.

"Way I hear it," Sonny continues, "couple of P.D.'s (public defenders) polished them off with guilty pleas. Ike got forty years. Homer ten."

"Who were the P.D.'s, Sonny? I must have been fishing in Canada or drunk when this happened."

"Rex Caldwell represented Ike."

"Ah, the Senator's boy. That figures."

"Three weeks ago Ike and Homer were released. State A. G.'s office said someone else killed Whitehall. Name of Underwood. His partner snitched on him. But those sons-a-bitches. They *knew* Ike and Homer didn't kill Whitehall."

"Where are Fellows and Kendrik now?" I ask, glaring at the Jack Daniels bottle.

"I don't know 'bout Kendrik, but Fellows is back in jail. You gotta see him, Luther. Help 'em nail the bastards who railroaded him."

"Yeah, right, Sonny, but I'm takin' some time off. Need to regroup, make some money. Fightin' city hall cases ain't worth much these days. Maybe I could find a good lawyer for them."

"Wait a minute," Sonny growls after a few minutes of silence. "Am I talkin' to Luther Parsons or someone who used to be him?"

"Sonny, I ain't no damn public defender," I reply. "This case sounds like a freebie. A few bucks at the best. Got no time for that. Too many other problems."

"Got no time, you crazy son of a bitch," Sonny threatens. "Well, you better find time, or I'll ram that Audi of yours right up your ass.

A click tells me Sonny's gone. Gazing up at a puffy cloud shaped like a dragon, I decide whether to return to Ohio is too tough a decision to make without a belt of Jack. For the umpteenth time since I re-habbed, temptation wins. One drink becomes two as I sail the Audi down Highway 77 at full throttle. Twenty minutes later, I sit on a bar stool at Mike's Pit Stop in Tracer, Arizona, and order a shot of Jack and Beer Nuts.

"Screw Sonny," I say too loud and a cute, busty blonde wearing an orange Jeff Gordon #24 T-shirt gives me the once-over. "Get this man a drink, Frank," she bellows, her right hand patting my shoulder.

Frank, whose right arm extends only to the elbow, obeys with Jack Daniels in hand. "Royce over there," he says pointing toward a cowboy hat at the end of the bar, "says you're famous. Are you famous?"

Raising my hand causes me to lose balance, but I manage to stand, wave at the cowboy hat, and say, "I used to be."

"Used to be" is good enough for my blonde benefactor and she snuggles up while Frank pours. Lack of any jewelry indicates I am a free man even though I'm not.

Ten minutes and four shots of JD later, I'm sitting cockeyed on the edge of the music stage telling war stories as a slow Willie Nelson favorite hums in the air. Surrounded by Olivia, the Gordon groupie, Frank, cowboy hat, and a cute waitress everyone calls Opie for a reason I cannot fathom, I weave tales true and false to my audience's delight.

"Shot him five times in the back?" cowboy hat asks while gulping a Red Rock.

"Dead straight," I answer, my words garbled in drunk talk.

"Bet the judge wet his pants," Opie offers.

"Yeah, when Thelma Ritter walked in that courtroom and began blasting away, Judge Harlor, ex-Marine if you will, jumped his ass to the side and behind the bench faster than one of those jackrabbits I nearly ran over on the way here. 'Course I didn't see it since I was across the hall repping some dude who stole French fries from a Burger King."

"How'd you get into the case?" Olivia asks, her hand comfortably on my knee.

"I heard the shots, five of them if I recall," I answer. "Early that evening Thelma's sister calls me and says Thelma needs help. I say, damn right she needs help, hell she just shot her ol' man in front of a damn judge and fifty witnesses. The sister, Roxy, if I remember right, then told me the story, one I told to the prosecutor and the detective two hours later."

"And that story was?" cowboy hat asks.

"At first, it looked like a dead end case, but the sister tells me that Thelma was upset after she watched her ol' man stomp to death her seventy-six year old father in a drunken stupor. Seems Brick, his nickname, was a mean mother, and somehow he got mad at Thelma's dad and started kicking him around. Thelma and her kids fought him, but he killed her dad."

"Police arrest him?" Olivia asks.

"Yeah, right on the spot, but the sister said Thelma brooded all night, couldn't sleep, just cried and cried. Next morning, she grabbed a .38 caliber revolver off the closet shelf and walked twenty-six blocks in ten degree temperature to the courthouse. Walked in Municipal Court #10 and blasted away."

"Then Brick got what he deserved," cowboy hat observes.

"Frontier justice, eye for an eye," Opie says. "They should have given her a freaking medal."

"A medal is not what Prosecutor James Darwin had in mind," I say. "He and the detective, Harry Dunn, wanted her to spend the rest of her life in jail. But when I took Roxy in with me and she told her story, both men cooled down."

"Where was Thelma all this time, after the killing, I mean?" Olivia asks.

"They took her to a mental hospital for observation," I answer. "Thought she must be crazy. After I talked with the prosecutor, I went to see her. Nice gal for a killer."

"How'd the case work out?" cowboy hat asks.

"The prosecutor and the detective agreed with a suggestion I made. I told them to let me take Thelma home; hell, she wasn't going to kill anyone else. Then we'd bury the case for a few months, keep it out of the press, and go from there. They said if I could get Judge Harlor to agree, it was fine with them. I saw him; he owed me a favor due to my representing the no-good son of a wrestler for free, and he said okay. I marched little Thelma, man, she probably didn't weigh much more than the .38 she'd held, right out of the Maynard R. Furguson Home For The Mentally Deranged, or something like that, and back to her loved ones. The neighbors cheered when we drove up. Brick was not a popular man.

"Didn't *Court TV* have something on about all this?" cowboy hat observes.

"Good memory. Year or so after the case was over, they used it on a special about vigilante justice. I got the meanest, nastiest letter from Brick's son about it. Man, was he pissed."

"And they had you on TV?" Olivia says, her hand rising from knee toward hip.

"Yeah, first time my mug was on the tube," I say, the words becoming more garbled as time passes.

"You really helped Thelma," Opie says. "Without you, she'd probably be in prison today."

"Poor folks always get the ass-end of things," cowboy hat adds. "Injustice and all that. Only thing that saves them is a good lawyer."

"Yeah, a good lawyer," I say while staring down at the whiskey shot in my left hand. "They're hard to find."

Chapter Three
Ike's Journey

When the words I have spoken about good lawyers being hard to find bothers me enough to poor my shot of Jack into a nearby cup full of cigarette butts and I decide Sonny's plea for help is worth the trip back to Ohio, I leave the Pit Stop and head for a hotel room to sober up. Olivia is game for bedroom action, and I disappoint her when I beg off. She shoves a business card imprinted with, "Olivia Sandberg, Tarot Cards My Specialty" in my hand and saunters off in a huff.

Nineteen hours and fifteen minutes later, the survivor of an electrical storm over Oklahoma that rivals every scene in *Twister* except the tornados, I sit in my Manchester law office across from Ike Fellows. He may be the latest edition of Thelma Brown, a man who needs someone in his corner fighting for his rights. Whether this is me I am about to discover.

"Can I do anything to these people, Mr. Parsons?" he asks so softly that I have to lean forward to hear him. "Can I do anything to them?"

"Just tell me what happened, Ike," I say impatiently. "Start at the beginning."

Ike Fellows rubs his forehead. A first impression of the shy, disfigured man is sadness. With his hands hidden in his pockets, he lumbered into my office like a man with an old war wound. There is a lingering foul smell that tells me he has not bathed in a week.

The lumps on Ike's face are blistery red, and his trembling hands are cracked and chapped. Laborer's hands. His stubby fingers are in constant motion; the man is a nervous breakdown in progress.

Despite Ike's appearance, I'm drawn to his gentle, pleading eyes. I call men like him "scabbers." Life's been a downhill slide since the day they were born.

Ike's younger sister Sharon is coiled up next to him. Like Ike, she's afflicted with genetic tumors. Her teeth are crooked, her hair uncombed. She looks exhausted, as if she's just finished working the night shift in a sweat shop.

"Go ahead, Ike. Take your time," I say, trying to put him at ease.

"After the Whitehall murder, I was selling pop bottles, but I heard they was lookin' for me so I called 'em," Ike mutters. "Police took me to the station. Said I shot some dude named Whitehall. I told 'em I didn't, but they kept sayin' I did. Told me Homer Kendrik said I did. I told 'em I didn't know him. They said some woman saw me at Whitehall's. I kept tellin' 'em I didn't know nothin' 'bout it."

"And who was the detective, Ike?" I ask.

"Hodges," he says, his voice barely audible.

"Detective Bud Hodges?"

"Yeah. He was nice at first, then he got mean."

Sharon pats Ike's hand. His eyes are watery, his parched lips twitching.

"Tell Mr. Parsons what they told you about *me*," she encourages, her hands trembling as she speaks.

"Mr. Hodges said he'd throw Sharon in jail and her kids in the state home. He told me I better tell the truth. I said I *was* telling the truth. That I didn't kill *nobody*. Mr. Hodges kept sayin' I did. He started throwin' things. Yellin'. Tellin' me not to be no fool. Callin' me stupid."

My fingers scramble to keep up with Ike's words. Page two of the yellow pad is full. My Mont Blanc runs out of ink. I grab a Bic Fine Line and tap it on the desk as Ike continues.

"I wanted him to quit yellin' so I told him I did it. Hodges went and got one of them recorders. Said to talk into it. He got real mad when I messed up 'cause he had to turn the recorder off. Then he'd tell me again what I was to say. Kept callin' me a dumb head. Told me what to say and I said it. Rogers was there, too. I was real scared, Mr. Parsons."

"Sheriff's Deputy Mike Rogers?" I ask.

"I guess," Ike replies.

"And Rogers was present when they took your statement?"

Ike nods and mumbles something I can't hear. Sharon's sobbing now, as if she is hearing this for the first time.

"I think I've got enough for now," I say. "Quite enough."

"Okay. Can I use the john?" Ike asks, his face drawn.

"Sure. Right around the corner. Down the hall."

When he's gone, Sharon fumbles through her purse and pulls out two wrinkled ten dollar bills.

"I got twenty dollars to give you if you'll help us," she says, pushing the money across the desk.

"Keep, keep that for now," I stammer. "At least until I can decide whether we've got a case."

Sharon stuffs the worn bills in her pocket and sits quietly waiting for her brother as I write a few more notes on the legal pad. I pull a file from the nearby credenza where I used to hide my bottles when I was on the booze train. Five minutes go by, then ten. There's no sign of Ike.

"Maybe I'd better check on your brother," I say.

Outside the bathroom, I call, "Ike, you okay?"

Hearing nothing, I push open the creaking door as the smell of vomit smacks my nasal passages. There's no light on. No sound. A flick of the light switch identifies a muddy work boot sticking out from beneath the stall door.

"Ike?" I say softening my tone. "You there?"

A faint sigh causes me to bend down and for a closer look. Ike is scrunched up against the wall in a fetal position to the left of the toilet. His trembling hands cover his face.

"You okay, Ike?" I ask kneeling down beside him.

Seconds go by, the only sound the drip, drip, drip of a faulty faucet.

"Ike. Ike. You okay?" I repeat.

"I ain't never goin' back," he says. "Never!"

I lean closer and touch his arm, but he jerks away.

"Here, Ike. Better wipe your chin."

"*Never* goin' back," he says, more convincing this time. "*Never*!"

I back off, trying to decide what to do. A tic under Ike's right eye activates.

"Ike, nobody's going to put you back in prison," I guarantee. "Now come on, let's get you out of here."

I extend my hand once again. He peers at me, his hollow eyes burning with rage. For a brief moment, I'm afraid he's going to charge up at me, knock me on my ass.

"Easy, Ike, easy," I beg backstepping.

A few uneasy seconds pass before Ike offers his quivering hand. He grasps mine tightly like a rock climber being helped up a steep ridge. I steady myself and help him to his feet.

Arm in arm, we walk down the hall toward my office as he wipes his soiled chin and shirt. He leans on me like I'm his last hope. When we finally reach the office, Ike slumps in the chair near Sharon. She reaches for him, gently patting his arm.

"It's okay, Ike," she assures him. "Mr. Parsons will help us."

"Hold on," I remind her. "I'm not sure I'm the right man for this case. This is a civil rights action and I don't specialize in that area."

"But you're a lawyer, aren't you, Mr. Parsons, and a real good one from what *I* hear."

"Well, thank you," I gasp, embarrassed. "Listen, you go home and get Ike some sleep and let me think about this. Then we'll talk again."

Ike starts to speak, but stops. Prison teaches a man to obey--no questions asked.

"Is there something else you wanted, Ike?" I say as he awkwardly rises from his chair and steadies himself.

Ike stares at the floor. "Can I do anything to these people, Mr. Parsons? Can I?" he utters.

I lean forward in my chair, trying to frame an answer.

"If everything adds up from what you've told me, *yes*, Ike, you can," I offer in a hesitant tone.

"Then you'll take our case, Mr. Parsons? You'll help us?" Sharon pleads.

"Hold on now. Like I said, let me give it some thought. I'll call you this evening."

Sharon's head drops at the sound of my words.

"Something wrong?" I ask.

"Mr. Parsons, me and Ike been to five lawyers. All of 'em said they'd be back to us, but none of 'em did."

"Listen, you be home around eight. I'll call you. I promise."

Minutes after Sharon and Ike leave, Sonny Burk stops by. I accept a Camel as we head out the door. An afternoon shower turning to drizzle awaits us.

"We got ourselves a new case, lawyer man?" Sonny asks.

"Not sure yet," I answer.

"Well, here's some reading material to help you decide," Sonny says while handing me a blue folder.

"Thanks, but . . ." I say but Sonny's ten feet away jumping a puddle as the rain pounds the pavement.

Inside the Audi, I wipe the raindrops off my glasses and open the file. Staring at me is the police report of Wesley Whitehall's murder. Prepared by Jerry Manweiller, a State Police crime scene expert, it reads:

> On Thursday, February 14, at 7:48 PM, Cpl. Steven Garcia, Post Commander, telephoned this officer at home. Cpl. Garcia advised that the Redding County Homicide Team was investigating a homicide at 1218 South 18th Street in Manchester. He advised that this officer was requested to go to the scene to assist in the investigation.
>
> This officer arrived at the scene at 9:46 PM. The scene was a two-story frame house, located on the east side of 18th Street. Yellow police line tape had been located around the front area of the residence.
>
> Several police officers were present upon my arrival. These officers were: Det. Oscar Fellows of Manchester Police Department, Officer Cal Porter of Redding County Sheriff's Department, and Deputy Coroner Forrest Simpkins. Det. Al Long of the State Police and Det. Bud Hodges of the Manchester Police Department arrived at the scene after the body had been removed to the coroner's office.
>
> The lower floor of the residence was divided in half by a hallway running from the front entrance door to a set of interior stairs leading to the upper story. The residence was divided into two apartments on the lower floor. Entry into

the apartment in which the victim was located was gained by going through a doorway at the east end of the above-mentioned hall. This apartment was on the south side of the residence.

This officer was advised that the call concerning this incident was received at approximately 6:45 PM. Det. Fellows advised that the kitchen light was the only light on when the first units arrived. The victim, who was lying on the kitchen floor, had a pillow over his head. This pillow had been removed from its original location and placed on top of a paper barrel just north of the victim's location.

Deputy Bill Jacobson photographed the scene using a video-cassette camera. He also took measurements at the scene for a crime scene sketch.

The interior of the residence was not well-kept. There were numerous items scattered about the apartment. The area was not clean. There was a strong odor of dog excrement and urine in the apartment. This officer was informed that there were three pit bull dogs locked in the basement. The door to the basement was located on the N. wall of the living room, and was secured by a hook and eye. The exterior door leading from the front porch to the hallway and the interior door leading from the hallway into the S. apartment both had damage in the area of the lock on the door leading into the apartment.

The victim was lying on the kitchen floor, stomach down, with his head toward the N.W. and his feet toward the S.E. He was lying so that the right side of his face was against the floor and his face was toward the S.W. The victim's right arm was on the floor and extended toward the N.W. His left hand was in a fist and was adjacent to the victim's forehead.

The victim was a white male with brown hair, wearing a black leather jacket with a fur collar, white sweatshirt, blue jeans and gray leather hiking boots. There was a gunshot wound to the left side of the victim's head. Adjacent to this wound there were what appeared to be white fibers. The victim had a massive wound to the frontal portion of his head.

There was a pool of coagulated blood under the victim's head and body. This pool of blood extended from 6" above the head to 6" below the waist. This blood had run in two streams from the head portion of the pool toward the N.E.

There was apparent brain tissue lying on the left forearm of the victim. This tissue apparently struck the front portion of the kitchen range approximately 10" up from the floor and then fell onto the arm.

There was an empty White Castle box against the base of the kitchen range and 8" N.W. of the victim's head. There was an unopened package of Doral cigarettes lying on the floor just to the S. of the victim's left elbow. An audio cassette tape "Wilson Phillips" and a paper with the words "Seized Cars" were laying on the floor near the victim's left elbow.

A fired Remington .12 gauge shotgun shell was lying against the victim's right side below the armpit. Adjacent to this shot gun shell and toward the E. was a plastic wallet-size photograph holder with photographs.

Approximately 25" E. of the victim's body there was a black leather wallet lying on the floor. A fired 9mm casing was lying on the floor N. of the victim's head.

A pillow covered by a pillowcase with the word GARFIELD and a caricature of a cat was lying on top of a stack of newspapers which were on top of a cardboard barrel. The pillow and pillowcase were just to the N. of the victim's body. The pillow and pillowcase had what appeared to be gunshot defects in them. There was hair and apparent blood on the item.

The victim's feet were against the base of a motor stand and the N.E. leg of a kitchen table which was located in the S.W. corner of the kitchen. On this kitchen table, there was a triple-beam balance-type scale and fragments of what appeared to be marijuana.

The following measurements were made using the South door between the kitchen and the living room as a reference point:

Top of victim's head	39" east and 10" south
Shot shell	58" east and 26" south
Photo insert	60" east and 24" south
Wallet	78" east and 32" south
Bottom of victim's right foot	63" east and 79" south
9mm fired casing	27" east and 29" north
Victim's left elbow	36" east and 29" south (against range)
N.E. corner of kitchen range	33" east and 6" south (36" wide)

Outside the kitchen, leaning against the W. wall of the living room was a .22 caliber rifle and a .12 gauge shotgun. Both of these weapons were covered with a heavy layer of undisturbed dust. A .25 caliber semi-automatic pistol was lying on the coffee table in the living room.

An empty, gray plastic pistol box was lying on a single bed in the living room. There were two folding Swiss Army knives on the coffee table in the living room. In the living room along the south wall, there was a telephone

answering machine and the base station for a cordless telephone. The telephone receiver was lying on top of a green parka-type coat. Numerous calls came into the residence during my investigation at the scene. Most callers did not leave a message on the answering machine. Det. Bud Hodges of the Manchester Police Department recovered the tape from the machine. This officer photographed the general scene using 35mm color process.
The body of the victim was removed from the scene at 12:31 AM by EMT personnel. Under the body this officer observed a 3"x3" clear plastic sheath (empty).
This officer left the scene at 12:54 AM. At 11:30 AM, this officer attended the autopsy of Wesley Whitehall, Jr. which was conducted at University Medical Center, Medical Science Building, Pathology Department, Cincinnati.
The autopsy was conducted by Dr. Gene Homerlin, head of forensics at the Medical Center. Also present were Det. Al Long, State Police and Det. Bud Hodges of Manchester Police Department, who identified the victim as Wesley Whitehall, Jr., Manchester, and Deputy Coroner Forest Simpkins. X-rays revealed as apparent entry wound in the brain area.
During the autopsy, it was determined that the victim had a gunshot entry wound in the left side of the head above the ear. This wound was a 7" long, slit-like wound with an apparent abrasion collar on the edge nearest the back of the head. The victim had an apparent gunshot exit wound in the area of the forehead which was irregularly shaped and measured approximately 3"x 3". Dr. Homerlin's opinion as to cause of death was: Single shotgun wound to the head.

Non-Fiction

Code of Silence,
Melvin Belli, Jack Ruby, and the Assassination of Lee Harvey Oswald

Prologue

When square-jawed Teamsters boss James Hoffa pressed the index finger of his left hand against his mouth while whispering, “Shhh,” Frank Ragano’s heart skipped a beat. Ever obedient, the Tampa, Florida mob attorney trailed the embattled union leader across the plush carpet of Hoffa's Washington D.C. office into an adjacent executive dining room. Little did attorney Melvin Belli, practicing law 2840 miles away in San Francisco, realize that the ensuing discussion between the powerful union boss and the prominent defense lawyer would indirectly catapult him into the most famous case of his career.

According to Ragano, his July 6, 1963 encounter with Hoffa on a musty day in the nation's capital marked a significant moment in Hoffa's continuing war with Robert Francis Kennedy. Ever since JFK's baby brother was appointed Attorney General, Hoffa was a marked man. Twenty prosecutors had been assigned under the auspices of what Hoffa's cronies dubbed the "Get Hoffa Squad." It had a singular purpose: convict Hoffa and imprison him.

Frank Ragano's entry into Hoffa's world had occurred in June of 1961, but the union leader became aware of the attorney's prowess through his balls-out representation of Cuban/American mobster Santo Trafficante, Jr. After gaining an acquittal of charges against the Mafia Don for tax evasion in Jacksonville, Florida, Ragano called the bluff of Hillsborough County Sheriff Ed Blackburn. He swore he would arrest Trafficante on the spot if he set foot in the Sheriff's fiefdom.

To test Blackburn's mettle, Ragano, a stocky man with a bulbous nose, puffy cheeks and deep set eyes, convinced Trafficante, who had accumulated wealth and power through narcotics trafficking, prostitution, and gambling, to risk arrest by accompanying him to the Sheriff's department. On May 10, 1960, the two men entered the building. Trafficante, a lean man with dangerous eyes, was briefly detained, but then promptly released when Ragano persuaded a friendly judge to threaten Blackburn with contempt. The tale of bravery in the line of fire earned Ragano his stripes with the Mafia. Trafficante's minions, knowledgeable that their boss called Ragano, "Che," dubbed the attorney, "Don Cheecho."

James Hoffa chuckled when he heard the story of Ragano's confrontation with Blackburn. When the Teamster's president was indicted in June of 1961 for racketeering in connection with the Sun Valley retirement home project near Cape Canaveral, the labor leader summoned Ragano to his side.

From word one, the two men discovered a common enemy: Robert F. Kennedy, whom Hoffa called "Booby." Ragano's distaste for RFK cemented a bond with Hoffa who detested the Attorney General. Hoffa told Ragano he had opposite feelings toward Santo Trafficante. "He's a classy guy. I'd like to meet him," Hoffa said.

Informed of the accolade, Trafficante returned the favor. "Tell Jimmy," the Mafioso told Ragano, "that I consider him a friend and that I hope he considers me a friend. If there is anything I can do for him I would be glad to do it." Ragano and Trafficante then agreed that in their presence they would call Hoffa, "Marteduzzo," Sicilian for, "Little Hammer."

Before the Sun Valley case was completed, Hoffa was indicted in Nashville, Tennessee for violating the Landrum-Griffin act. It forbid union leaders from accepting payoffs from employers in return for sweetheart contacts. The government alleged Hoffa had benefited through payoffs to Test Fleet, a Flint, Michigan based leasing company owned by Hoffa and his wife. The trial resulted in a hung jury. Jury tampering was suspected.

During the Test Fleet trial, Ragano learned of another figure who played a prominent role in the future of Melvin Belli. He was Carlos Marcello, the feared Don of New Orleans and a close friend of Santo Trafficante. Within months, Ragano added Marcello, whose flat nose, swept back oiled hair, and ever present sunglasses provided the perfect image for a Mafia poster boy, to his *client* list. That occurred after he impressed the "Big Daddy in the Big Easy" with his savvy regarding a pending Louisiana indictment against James Hoffa.

Like Hoffa, Marcello, born in Tunesia (his parents were Sicilian) as Calogero Minacore, possessed a hatred of Robert Kennedy, who had targeted the Mafioso for extinction during the early days of the new administration. The New Orlean's Don's fury was exacerbated when Kennedy directed a brief deportation of Marcello to Guatemala. Following the embarrassment, the short, stocky mobster vowed revenge. After a dinner in March of 1963 attended by Ragano, Trafficante and Marcello, the latter said, "It's a goddamn shame what the Kennedys are putting Jimmy through." "Yes," Trafficante agreed, "If Kennedy hadn't been elected, Jimmy never would have been indicted."

In between sips of steaming coffee, Marcello continued the discussion, saying, "You, Jimmy, and me are in for hard times as long as Bobby Kennedy is in office. Someone ought to kill that son-of-a-bitch. That Bobby Kennedy is making life miserable for me and my friends. Someone ought to kill *all* of those Kennedys."

Later than evening, Trafficante mentioned to Ragano his distaste for the Kennedy's due to their hypocrisy. "Here's this guy, Bobby Kennedy, talking about law and order, and these guys made their goddamn fortune through bootlegging, " he said in a reference to Joseph Kennedy's bootlegging operations. Trafficante then added, "Bobby Kennedy is stepping on too many toes. Che, you wait and see, somebody is going to kill those sons-of-bitches. It's just a matter of time."

The fate of the President was debated in front of Ragano in another Florida city shortly after his dinner with Trafficante, whom Ragano described "as close to me as a brother," and Marcello. This occurred in Hoffa's $1000 per night suite at the Edgewater Beach Hotel in Miami. Among those attending was Hoffa, attorney Bill Bufalino, Joey Glimco, head of Chicago cabdrivers' Local 777, and Ragano.

As a rigorous gin rummy game proceeded amidst idle chatter, Glimco, who had battled RFK during a Senate hearing into racketeering, blurted, "What do you think would happen if something happened to Bobby Kennedy?" Buffalino retorted, " . . . John Kennedy would be so pissed off, he would probably replace him with someone who would be more of a son-of-a-bitch than Bobby."

The thought lingered in the smoke-filled room until James Hoffa spoke up. "Suppose something happened to the president, instead of Bobby?" he said. Buffalino answered, "Lyndon Johnson would get rid of Bobby."

"Damn right he would," Hoffa exclaimed. "He hates him as much as I do. Don't forget, I've given a hell of a lot of money to Lyndon in the past."

In May of 1963, two months after Hoffa's statement, he was indicted for jury tampering. A month later, the union leader was indicted in New Orleans for "looting $25 million in fraudulent funds from the pension fund" in connection with loans made to the Fountainbleau Hotel. The charges escalated the harsh feelings Hoffa, Trafficante, and Marcello possessed for RFK, and his older brother.

Evidence of Hoffa's personal hatred for Robert Kennedy surfaced shortly thereafter. According to Ragano, RFK had agreed to be present during a meeting in Washington, D.C., where government prosecutors presented documents critical to the prosecutions of Hoffa. The union boss decided to accompany his attorneys to the confab, but when they arrived, RFK was absent.

Hoffa fumed at the slight while Ragano sifted through the documents. Forty-five minutes later, the Attorney General sauntered through the door accompanied by a large dog on a leash.

"Where the hell do you get off keeping me waiting while you're walking your dog," Hoffa roared. "I've got a lot of important people to see."

Kennedy ignored the testy words, spouting, "I'm in charge, not you." Without hesitation, Hoffa lunged at Kennedy and started choking him. "You son of a bitch," he screamed. "I'll break your neck. I'll kill you."

Ragano swore he and his colleagues had to pry Hoffa's beefy fingers from RFK's throat. Seconds later, the Attorney General, without so much as a word, marched out of the room dog in tow.

Hoffa's frame-of-mind, Ragano reported, was predictable. "After his encounter with Kennedy," the lawyer said, "Jimmy was increasingly distraught, his temper at a lower-than-usual flashpoint."

The subsequent July 23, 1963 meeting with Hoffa at his headquarters caused Ragano to realize that his client had passed the talking stage. When they were alone in the executive dining room, the attorney recalled, "Jimmy drew his chair close to mine and in a muffled voice asked when I intended to see Santo and Carlos."

Ragano answered that he was leaving that evening for New Orleans to meet with the twin Mafioso. Hoffa's face lit up as he said to his lawyer, "The time has come for your friend and Carlos to get rid of him, kill that son-of-a-bitch John Kennedy."

Ragano's mind-set was immediate. "For a second I thought I had misheard him," he said. "and I was unable to conceal the astonishment that he must have read in my face. But he stared penetratingly into my eyes, with a fiercely determined gaze."

According to Ragano, Hoffa then said, "This has got to be done. Be sure to tell them what I said. No more screwing around. We're running out of time-something has got to be done."

True to his command, Ragano delivered the message to Trafficante and Marcello. One hundred and forty-nine days later, on the afternoon of November 22, 1963, John Fitzgerald Kennedy, the 35th President of the United States, was assassinated. Two days later, JFK's alleged killer, Lee Harvey Oswald, was gunned down by Dallas stripclub owner, Jack Ruby. Within days, attorney Melvin Belli was hired to represent Oswald's assassin.

Two years after the "Trial of the Century" that produced a guilty as charged verdict against Ruby, Frank Ragano sued *Time Magazine* for libel in connection with a photograph whose caption intimated that he was a member of the Mafia.

To represent him, Ragano hired Belli as co-counsel despite his having no expertise with libel cases.

During a conversation regarding his new attorney with Santo Trafficante, Ragano's ears perked up when the aging mobster's face became rigid. After Trafficante said, "I'm surprised he [Belli] would take your case," he added, "Che, whatever you do, don't ask him about Jack Ruby. It's none of your business."

Ragano heeded his client's advice, and never discussed the Ruby case with Belli even though the two high-profile attorneys developed a lasting friendship. Four decades later, new information would surface that shed light on why Santo Trafficante warned Ragano to avoid the Ruby subject. When it was addressed, allegations surfaced that Melvin Belli was recruited by the mob to discredit, and in effect, silence Jack Ruby thus becoming an active co-conspirator in the cover-up following the assassinations of John F. Kennedy and Lee Harvey Oswald.

Book I

Chapter One
Preliminaries

"Candid, Controversial, and Clever, Lawyer Melvin Belli is a Perry Mason with Showmanship." So had read the headline text above an *Associated Press* article describing the fifty-seven-year-old San Francisco attorney. The same one who stepped out of a fancy automobile in front of the Dallas, Texas County Courthouse on February 18, 1964. The eight story building, built in 1913 by architect H.A. Overbeck in the classic "NeoColonial" architectural style, it featured marble staircasing through the entrance at the corners of Houston and Main Street in downtown Dallas.

Flashbulbs popped, frenzied reporters shouted questions, and police manhandled a boisterous crowd as Belli, a briefcase in one hand, his trademark black Homburg in the other, stepped lively up the steps. Inside, Judge Joseph Brantley Brown, a gray-haired gent whose favorite companion was an ever-present pipe, prepared to convene what the media dubbed, "The Trial of the Century."

To be determined was the fate of Jacob Rubenstein, a/k/a Jack Ruby, the snaky strip-club owner charged with gunning down suspected President John Fitzgerald Kennedy assassin Lee Harvey Oswald in the only live television broadcast of a murder in history. A jury of Ruby's peers would decide if he was guilty of first-degree murder, or not guilty by reason of insanity. If the former were decided, death by electrocution was likely.

The entry of the flamboyant Belli into the Ruby case added to the Hollywood atmosphere surrounding the trial. The most famous lawyer in the world was a headline-maker who had been the subject of a recent *Los Angeles Times* article by Jack Smith that bore the banner, "L.A. Watching New Court Idol Emerge."

Several publications were more interested in Belli's fashion statement than in his prowess as an attorney. *Time Magazine* applauded his "Chesterfield overcoat with fur collar." *The Saturday Evening Post* described his tailor as having "added certain nonconformist modifications. The jacket and matching vest are lined with bright red silk, and the pockets of the sharply creased trousers are cut parallel to the waist, frontier style."

Washington Post reporter Bill Flynn focused on the overall "Belli look." He described the lawyer's fondness for "Saville Row suits, handmade shirts with diamond studs, flowing Byronesque ties, starched cuffs, and polished high-heeled black boots." Famed reporter Dorothy Kilgallen, a steady lunch partner of Belli's during the trial who later mysteriously died of a drug overdose, observed, "The Carl Sandburgs of the future will spend whole lifetimes trying to analyze the drama of this week and this scene." She described Belli's demeanor as "Chesterfieldian."

When the dapper lawyer from San Francisco dodged eager reporters and entered the packed courtroom, onlookers whispered, "There's Melvin Belli," and pointed. The barrister was every bit the media star his client had become.

Jailer Al Maddox, who booked Jack Ruby into jail following his arrest for killing Oswald, recalled that Belli was "very gracious, had a lot of class. He was oozing with intelligence and knowledge. I'd put him and Jack in a room and let them talk."

As Belli stood beside Jack Ruby, court observers noted the differences in the two men. Belli, though short in stature, was a commanding figure, his bulk noticeable. Black-horned rimmed glasses perched on an oversized nose were encased on a square set jaw. Swept-back wavy silver-hair parted to the right exposed bushy eyebrows and a furrowed brow that belied a man oozing with confidence. When he made a point, he cradled his glasses in his right hand and thrust them forward as if to say, "Now, listen closely or you'll miss something important."

In contrast, fifty-one-year-old Jack Ruby (some said he was fifty-two) bore a small frame (5'9", 175 pounds). He seemed to have shrunk in size since his arrest eighty-six days earlier. His face was nondescript, his expression nonchalant like that of a retired uncle whose hairline had receded as life passed him by. He spoke in a high-pitched tone with a slight lisp, a trait that caused some to dub him a "sissy." Al Maddox, the jailer who had booked him into the Dallas County jail after he shot Oswald, called him, "a used to be."

If Lee Harvey Oswald's killer possessed any distinguishing characteristic, it was his eyes—ones that appeared hollow like killer's eyes. Belli, whose green eyes sparkled when he became excited, said, "There was something about [Ruby's] eyes. They shone like a beagle's."

Belli and Ruby were featured performers in the February 21, 1964 issue of *Life Magazine*. Featuring the infamous and controversial photograph of Lee Harvey Oswald brandishing his rifle on the cover, the magazine touted headlines reading, "Exclusive—Oswald Armed For Murder, In Full And Extra Ordinary

Detail, The Life Of The Assassin." Below the caption, the blurb read, "As Jack Ruby Goes To Trial, Cast Of Characters; How The Law Applies."

If Belli wanted the world to believe Ruby was insane, the two-page vertical photograph of Jack on pages 26 and 27 must have pleased him. Ruby stood with his hands clasped in handcuffs in a dark suit, white shirt and tie. His eyes blankly stared at the reader in an eerie fashion. To Belli's apparent delight, the photograph caption read, "As Ruby goes to trial, the question before the court: Was This Man Sane?" Readers were informed that, "this extraordinary picture of Jack Ruby was taken as he was leaving jail for pretrial tests by doctors to examine the physical and mental condition of the man who shot Lee Harvey Oswald."

In the second paragraph of the story, Belli was described as "a Californian with a fantastic record of courtroom victories." His counterpart D.A. Henry Wade, when asked about the insanity defense, stated, "We think it is a case of cold-blooded, calculated murder."

Pages 28 and 29 featured five photographs of Jack Ruby during various stages of his life. He was depicted in Army uniform holding hands with a woman friend (1944), as a "song and dance man" tapping his feet with a young dancer named Sugar Daddy (1957), alongside sister Eva, and at the moment when he approached Oswald gun-ready for assassination. The final photograph—a page-and-a-half wide, featured Ruby, dapperly dressed in black suit, white shirt, and white tie with gold tie-clasp, smiling, head-cocked, with two of his Carousel Nightclub strippers. Scantily clad, they were positioned on both sides facing Ruby, legs and bikini bottoms in full view. A portion of the caption read that Ruby was "basking in the attention of two of his strippers."

At pages 32 and 33, the "Cast Of The Courtroom Drama" was presented. Belli standing in his famous office flanked by law books and a brick wall peppered with memorabilia, points to his right as if he is addressing a jury. Replete in a spiffy tie and suit sporting a lengthy gold pocket watch chain, he is glasses-less as he makes a point. In the smaller photographs alongside is his chief prosecutor Henry Wade, Assistant D.A. Bill Alexander, and presiding Judge Joe Brown.

Tugging at a cigar stuffed into the right corner of his mouth, Wade, wearing black horn-rimmed glasses imbedded in his eye sockets, is puffy-faced while chatting on the telephone. The caption mentions that Wade's office won 189 felony trials and lost only thirteen in 1963.

The photograph of Brown indicates a strong similarity to Wade, described by jailer Al Maddox as "a good old country boy. Sheriff Decked liked him and if the one-eyed sheriff liked someone, then he had to be all right." Brown wears black horned rimmed glasses and sweeps his curly hair back like Wade. Only a bit more bulbous nose separated the two in appearance.

Left out of the photographs was Belli's 300-pound co-counsel, Joe Tonahill. A native of Hot Springs, Texas with an expertise in personal injury law, Tonahill, like Belli, did not possess experience with criminal defense. "Tonahill did not belong in the case," Bill Alexander told the author. "He was a big, bullfrog of a guy, a bullshit artist who liked to overpower people with his size and his voice. I guess he was chosen since he was a personal injury lawyer buddy of Belli's and because he was from Texas, but he was from the southeast part, not Dallas and that didn't help the defense any."

As jury selection approached, Belli and Tonahill knew they faced an uphill battle. Their client had committed murder not just in front of one, or two, or ten witnesses, but millions who sought a glimpse of the alleged killer of their beloved President on national television. Instead they recoiled in horror as the Dallas strip-club owner shot and killed Lee Harvey Oswald in cold blood.

Several options appeared open to Belli regarding his representation of Ruby. He could attempt to strike a plea bargain with the prosecution, plead his client guilty, and throw Oswald's killer on the mercy of the court hoping for sympathy. It was discarded, Belli said, because District Attorney Henry Menasco Wade, later to gain more fame when he was the "Wade" in the momentous "Roe vrs. Wade" abortion case, had decided that Ruby would be prosecuted to the full extent of the law.

Belli's second option involved essentially pleading Ruby guilty while arguing special circumstances the lawyer hoped would convince a jury Ruby deserved to be spared the death penalty. Belli's legal colleagues urged that line of defense, but Belli ignored it for reasons known only to him.

The defense chosen was "not guilty by reason of insanity," but it was risky. Despite being a recognized excuse for criminal conduct, Belli knew most juries disliked the plea since it permitted a guilty man to go free based on a "technicality." Regardless, Belli was determined to base his defense on "psychomotor epilepsy," a condition that could excuse Ruby's conduct. Every member of the defense team and his legal colleagues in San Francisco tried to discourage the strategy believing it ill-fated, but that didn't deter the stubborn Belli.

Complicating Belli's task was another matter—one he alleged overshadowed all else. The defense counsel believed that no jury in Dallas, or in Texas, for that matter, could provide his client a fair trial. To that end, he had argued that it was impossible for any juror to be impartial, since everyone knew Ruby shot Oswald. Furthermore, Belli said, the citizens of Dallas had been embarrassed over the shooting of the President, and sending Ruby to the electric chair would be a means to closure. All while showing the world that there was indeed justice in the Lone Star State.

The makeup of the Dallas population concerned Belli. Never one to hold back his feelings, he bellowed, "Dallas was a city of hate, a city where Adlai Stevenson [October 24, 1963 during "United Nations Day"] was spat upon and hit on the head with a picket sign and where the American flag was hung upside-down by General Edwin Walker, a man relieved of his command in Germany for indoctrinating his troopers in the right-wing extremism of the John Birch Society." He added "[Dallas] was a city where the 'Minutewoman' would get on the telephone and call all over with such messages as 'Mental health is Communistic' and 'Fluoridation is a Communist plot.' And this was not just a lunatic fringe, this was the prevailing mood of the Dallas oligarchy that ran the town and told it what to think."

Later, Federal Judge Sarah Hughes agreed with Belli's assessment. She called Dallas, "The only American city in which the President could have been shot." Reporters dubbed Dallas, "Murder capital of the world," "A sick city," "A festering sore," and "A city of shame and hate."

If lack of a viable defense for Ruby and a prevailing mood of hatred toward him by the citizens of Dallas wasn't enough, Belli believed he faced a judge bent on executing Jack Ruby. Regarding Judge Brown, Belli would later conclude, ". . . He was weak and he let the District Attorney make his decisions for him, because he knew he was too ignorant of the law to make many decisions on his own."

Bolstering his point about Judge Brown's lack of competence, Belli pointed out that the judge had never graduated from high school, that he attended what the barrister called "a third rate law school, practiced law for one year, became a justice of the peace, and two decades later was appointed to the criminal court."

Belli's favorite story regarding Judge Brown involved an early ruling that called for the judge to check case law and the application of a basic legal term, "res gestae." Belli swore that Judge Brown summoned him to the bench, and then said, "Mel, I wish you'd lay off that pig Latin."

In later articles, Belli accused Judge Brown of being a racist. Ruby's lawyer said that when he mentioned several cases that supported his plea that Oswald's killer be released on bail, Judge Brown whispered, "Mel, them's nigger cases. Don't cite 'em."

JFK assassinations expert Mary Farrell defended Brown, who she said, "dated' the same "blonde" that Belli did during the case. "In Texas in the 1960s," Farrell said, "judges were not noted for being PhD's on the bench. They were ordinary people but that was okay. Not Harvard or Yale, but smart men with good common sense."

Jailer Maddox confirmed Farrell's passion for women. "He loved them," Maddox said. "On one occasion, he went out with the wife of a restaurant owner. When the affair was exposed, the guy killed his wife. He never spent a day in jail."

Preparation for the Jack Ruby trial caused Belli to brush up on recent history. He was especially aware of the contentious atmosphere that prevailed in Dallas during the months of 1963 leading up to the fall.

Lee Harvey Oswald, the man who police alleged killed John Fitzgerald Kennedy, wasn't the only one in Dallas apparently upset with the President. Animosity toward JFK, the youngest President ever elected, was apparent prior to this ill-fated visit in November of 1963. Symbolic of the mood was a local minister's comment. He told his parishioners during the previous election, "If you vote for that Catholic Kennedy, don't ever come to my church again."

Dislike for President Kennedy was a given among many Americans. Certain groups disliked his religious background, or his stand on racial issues, but much of the disdain for the nation's chief executive among rank and file union workers and their leaders had its roots in the actions of brother Bobby, whose first public feud began while JFK was a Senator from Massachusetts. It involved the investigation of Teamster's Union leaders Dave Beck and James Hoffa.

When Beck was forced to step down as president of the union, Hoffa ruled. Robert Kennedy launched a personal crusade to end his rein based on his belief that Hoffa was mob related. The investigation, undertaken by a Senate subcommittee that included JFK, probed the Teamsters as never before. This

despite warnings from family patriarch Joseph Kennedy that Jack's political future would be harmed.

In the months prior to the fall of 1963, Belli knew the Kennedy administration had weathered considerable storms. Skirmishes due the civil rights movement in the south caused them to support desegregation efforts. Bloody incidents blemished the transition and Robert Kennedy became a hated man among those who believed Negroes deserved, among other things, to be seated in the back of the bus and use separate toilet facilities than the whites.

After the Kennedys supported Martin Luther King's freedom march on Washington, applauded his "I Have A Dream" speech, and worked with civil rights leaders to upgrade their rights, the Kennedy brothers faced a crucial crisis in American history. Together they avoided war even though Russian premiere Nikita Krushchev deployed missiles to Cuba. Behind the scenes negotiations between RFK and Soviet counterpart Anatoly Dobrynin saved the world from a nuclear holocaust.

As November of 1963 approached, John Kennedy realized he needed to mend political fences in Texas, where rumors of a rift between Senator Ralph Yarborough and Governor John Connally existed. It threatened to prevent the President from winning the state in the 1964 election. A trip to Texas including a stop in Dallas, Belli discovered, was thus planned.

On November 21, 1963, JFK and Jackie flew to Texas after they attended a gala party celebrating Robert Kennedy's thirty-eighth birthday. Before leaving on the Texas trip, Jack Kennedy made plans with his brother to attend the upcoming Harvard-Yale football game. Two days later, Bobby was at home eating lunch poolside with United States Attorney Robert Morgenthau when he was summoned to the telephone at 1:45 p.m. The caller was FBI director J. Edgar Hoover, a bitter rival of Bobby's, who said, "I have news for you. The president has been shot. I think it's serious . . . "

Minutes later, Hoover called back and said four words that permeated Robert Francis Kennedy's brain like a spear. He said, "The president is dead." Robert had lost a brother; the nation had lost its 35th President. At 2:38, Lyndon Baines Johnson became the 36th President of the United States.

The murder of John Kennedy and the subsequent killing of his assassin Lee Harvey Oswald by Jack Ruby resulted in Melvin Belli's appearance in the case. Later, he admitted that he was apprehensive about his safety during the trial. He said he was advised to keep out of sight, but in pure Belli style, he and Tonahill, son-in-law of conservative Virginia congressman Howard K. Smith, paraded down the main streets like they were tourists.

Ruby's counsel refused a request from the county sheriff to provide security, but he later told *Playboy Magazine*, "I'm going to tell you the truth. I was scared shitless. I used to say, despite all my enemies, that no one would ever actually want to shoot me. But after walking down the street and seeing the hate in the eyes of everyone who watched, I never would say that again."

Most lawyers faced with the insurmountable odds of defending a client under the circumstances that Belli encountered would have withdrawn their representation and left Ruby's fate in the hands of a public defender or another competent attorney. But Melvin Mouron Belli was certainly not "most lawyers," for from the very day he earned the right to practice law, he had been a crusader for the rights of the downtrodden, a champion of the underdog, like no one before him.

With those lofty credentials in tow, Belli swore during the first press conference he conducted in Dallas that Jack Ruby would be afforded every right guaranteed him under the Constitution. Long after the trial was over, questions would linger as to whether the bombastic barrister had achieved that goal or had other, more diabolical, motives in mind.

Regardless, when Judge Brown pounded his gavel to quiet noisy spectators and begin "The Trial of the Century," Belli was determined that justice would prevail. Twenty-five days later, he would scream to the high heavens that it had not.

Book Reference List

The Purpose Driven Life, Rick Warren

Into Thin Air, Jon Krakauer

Tropic of Cancer, Henry Miller

1984, George Orwell

A Farewell to Arms, Ernest Hemingway

Seabiscuit, Laura Hillenbrand

Moby Dick, Herman Melville

A Time to Kill, John Grisham

Presumed Innocent, Scott Turow

The Road Not Taken, Robert Frost

Misery, Stephen King

How Stella Lost Her Groove, Terry McMillan

Grapes of Wrath, John Steinbeck

The Great Gatsby, F. Scott Fitzgerald

Gone with the Wind, Margaret Mitchell

Truman, David McCullough

The Best and the Brightest, David Halberstram

The Old Man and the Sea, Ernest Hemingway

Tuesdays with Morrie, Mitch Albom

Down and Out in London and Paris, George Orwell

Harry Potter and the Sorcerer's Stone, J. K. Rowling

Miscarriage of Justice, The Jonathan Pollard Story, Mark Shaw

Leaves of Grass, Walt Whitman

The Hunt for Red October, Tom Clancy

Kiss the Girls, James Patterson

Bibliography

Atlas Shrugged, Ayn Rand, Signet, New York, 1992

Balzac and the Little Chinese Seamstress, Dai Sijie, Anchor Books, New York, 2001

Blessings, Anna Quindlen, Random House, New York, 2002

Centennial, James A. Michener, Random House, 1974

Dead Man's Walk, Larry McMurtry, Simon and Schuster, New York, 1995

Down and Out in Paris and London, George Orwell, Harcourt, New York, 1933

Elements of Style, William Strunk, Jr. and E. B. White, Longman, New York, 2000

Focus on Grammar, Marjorie Fuchs, Longman, New York, 1994

Gone with the Wind, Margaret Mitchell, Warner, New York, 1939

Interview with the Vampire, Ann Rice, Ballantine, New York, 1976

Lapsing into a Comma, Bill Walsh, Contemporary Books, Chicago/New York, 2000

Daddy's Little Girl, Mary Higgins Clark, Pocket, New York, 2002

M Is for Malice, Sue Grafton, Ballantine, New York, 1996

Moby Dick, Herman Melville, Penguin, New York, 2003

Presumed Innocent, Scott Turow, Warner Books, New York, 1987

Seeing Scarlet, Barbara Kingsolver, Small World, Harper Collins, New York, 2002

Sleep No More, Greg Isles, Penguin, New York, 2003

The AP Stylebook, Associated Press, New York, 2000

The Catcher in The Rye, J. D. Salinger, Little, Brown, New York, 1945

The Complete Idiot's Guide to Grammar and Style, Laurie E. Rozakis, Alpha Books, Indianapolis, 1997

The Deep End of the Ocean, Jacquelyn Mitchard, Penguin, New York, 1996

The Dreyfus Affair and Other Writings, Emile Zola, Yale University Press, New Haven and London, 1996

The Firm, John Grisham, Random House, New York, 1991

The Old Man and the Sea, Ernest Hemingway, Charles Scribner's Sons, New York, 1952

The Portable James Joyce, Edited by Harry Levin, Penguin Books, New York, 1976

The Second Time Around, Mary Higgins Clark, Simon and Schuster, 2003

The Short Stories of John Steinbeck, Viking Press, New York, 1953

To Kill A Mockingbird, Harper Lee, Perennial Classics, New York, 2002

Villa Incognito, Tom Robbins, Bantam, 2003

We Were The Mulvaneys, Joyce Carol Oates, Plume, New York, 1996

Notes

Notes

To Order Copies of Grammar Report, Book Report, Poetry Report, My Book Proposal, or DVD Copies of Mark Shaw's "How To Become A Published Author or Poet: A to Z Seminars:"

Telephone Books For Life Foundation at 970-544-3398

E-mail at help@booksforlifefoundation.com,

Visit Books For Life Foundation at 450 South Galena Street, Aspen, Colorado

Write Books For Life Foundation at P. O Box CC, Aspen, Colorado 81611

Seminars, Speaking Engagements

Mark Shaw and other Books For Life Foundation staff members and advisors are available to conduct seminars focusing on writing tips, publishing strategies, and storytelling ideas at high schools, colleges, universities, libraries, writer's centers, writer's groups, youth groups, senior centers, corporations, and legal organizations. For more information, visit www.booksforlifefoundation.com.

Heidi Newman – Proofreading and Copyediting Services Contact Information: Telephone 317-818-8189, email – proofreader@ameritech.net

Mark Shaw

Mark Shaw is a former lawyer turned author with fourteen published books. They include *Book Report, Grammar Report, Poetry Report, From Birdies To Bunkers, Miscarriage of Justice, Let The Good Times Roll, The Jonathan Pollard Story, Larry Legend, Testament To Courage, The Perfect Yankee, Bury Me In A Pot Bunker,* and *Forever Flying.*

Mr. Shaw is a literary consultant, and creative director of Books For Life Foundation. Along with his canine pal, Black Sox, he lives in Aspen Colorado. More about Mark Shaw and contact information is available at www.markshaw.com or www.booksforlifefoundation.com

Printed in the United States
16622LVS00004B/415-450